T0198583

One More Rhyme for the
Road

One More Rhyme for the Road

Sue A. McLaughlin

iUniverse®

ONE MORE RHYME FOR THE ROAD

iUniverse books may be ordered through booksellers or by contacting:

iUniverse
1663 Liberty Drive
Bloomington, IN 47403
www.iuniverse.com
1-800-Authors (1-800-288-4677)

Because of the dynamic nature of the Internet, any web addresses or links contained in this book may have changed since publication and may no longer be valid. The views expressed in this work are solely those of the author and do not necessarily reflect the views of the publisher, and the publisher hereby disclaims any responsibility for them.

Any people depicted in stock imagery provided by Getty Images are models, and such images are being used for illustrative purposes only. Certain stock imagery © Getty Images.

ISBN: 978-1-5320-9949-6 (sc)
ISBN: 978-1-5320-9950-2 (e)

Print information available on the last page.

iUniverse rev. date: 05/08/2020

Contents

I. Lighthearted

II. Occasions

III. God's World

IV.   About Me

V.   Pensive

VI.   Health and Happiness

VII. About Heaven

VIII. About Him

IX.   Readin', Writin', No 'Rithmetic

SECTION I

A.D.D.

Attention Deficit Disorder—that's what the letters stand for.
We just called it "hyper", back in my day.
You didn't hear much back then of A.D.D.,
And folks like that were just "that way".

As I am older, I've discovered
That my mind really has A.D.D.
But my body seems to have developed
A major case of Slow Moving Disorder—S.M.D.

Maybe Sedentary, Slowing Down, Syndrome?
Or "I just can't do what I used to do" disease.
I've finally figured it all out—my brain has A.D.D.
But the rest of me is slow—it's such a tease!

My mind races ninety-to-nothing
Around and around till I'm quite dotty.
Planning, scheming, moving, dreaming,
But all the while bound within my slow body.

I wish I could, I should have, I could have,
I want to, I will—all playing in my head.
I must move that, or do this, or figure this out—
Then I realize that I am lying in my bed.

Being Grownup Sucks!

I am long past the age of innocence,
Eons away from what I used to portray,
No longer can I claim "I didn't know",
Or any more pretend naiveté.

I every day must claim adulthood,
There's no way around it, I really am stuck.
Childhood is a very long time past,
But still I cry, "Being grownup sucks!"

I so wish I was a youngun once more.
I detest being among the muckety-mucks.
No matter what anyone says,
Being grownup sucks!

How I'd love to curl up on my Mother's lap,
Stick my thumb in my mouth and cuddle.
But that's not to be, I'm grown-up, don't you see,
And life is a terrible muddle.

If I could only insist on a do-over,
I know I'd be great and have a million bucks;
But I can't and I don't and I didn't,
And being grownup sucks!

Change for You

Painting abstracts is my forte
Living abstractly is my life.
Could you love me if I changed my hair?
Would you, then, become my wife?

What can I do to make you love me?
Maybe my appearance isn't to your liking.
Maybe you'd rather I be clean-shaven.
I think if I wore a tuxedo I'd be quite striking.

Do you want me to change my job?
Should I be an ambassador or baker or banker?
Maybe a doctor or dentist or Indian Chief
Is for what you secretly hanker?

I want to know what I could do—
I know I really sound needy.
Tell me, please, if I must change for you.
I know, I must appear greedy.

Well, if you don't know, how can I change?
How can I help my case here?
Well, if I have to change all that much
I'm leaving you, my dear.

Childhood Games

"Liar, liar, pants on fire"—you've said that once, I bet
"Nanny, nanny, boo-boo"—what's not to get?
"All-y, All-y ins all free"—when did you say that
Or some similar version you've chanted from the past?

Do you remember childhood, skipping rope and such?
All the famous skipping chants you loved so much?
Step on a crack, you'll break your Mother's back,
Or all the fun you had with just a stick or a sack?

Do you even remember "Hide and Seek"
Or "Red Rover" or "King of the Hill"?
"Tag", "Kick the Can", and "Hopscotch"?
Think back and I bet you will.

Shooting marbles or playing with paper dolls,
"Jacks" and "Pick Up Sticks"?
Just what did you play as a young child,
Just how did you "get your kicks"?

Perhaps you were more into "Checkers"
"Dominoes", "Tinker Toys", "Chess"?
Or board games like "Clue" or "Memory"
Were more fun for you, yes?

Then there was, of course, "Monopoly"
A million games have come after.
"Sorry", "Parcheesi", "Chutes and Ladders"—
Anything that brought pleasure and laughter.

Just stop for a minute, remember them,
But don't shed a tear for the past.
The games and the phrases of childhood
Are just mem'ries—the die is cast.

Chocolate!

Now that's something I can sink my teeth into!
The incredible, edible Chocolate!
Hot or cold, milk or dark or mocha,
With nuts of any kind, or peanut butter;
Orange cream, butter cream, praline, nonpareil,
Fudge, brownies, cookies, chocolate chips,
Nougat, crunchy, s'mores or simply melted;
Marshmallow-filled or cherries in the center,
I am making myself hungry—this is pathetic!
Especially if you happen to be diabetic!

Discombobulated

I can work on my computer for a couple of hours
Before beginning to get discombobulated.
I attempt to pen a poem, but lose my train of thought,
And, before I know it, I'm twitter-pated.
I'm gung-ho pursuing a brand-new project,
But my brain hasn't completely accommodated.

What a strange feeling, this discombobulation!
Not good, not bad, not pensiveness nor elation.
As they say, it is what it is— a different sensation,
Not something that's familiar, there's no relation.
Is everyone affected in His whole creation?
Sometimes I liken it to a temporary tintinnabulation!

Don't Die

Don't die on a week day
I've got too much to do;
My schedule's just so busy
I don't have time for you.
Don't die on a Saturday,
I need to go grocery shopping,
And I promised to take the kids to the park—
They really keep me hopping.
Not a Sunday, for goodness sake—
It's so full with church and dinner;
I really couldn't miss it
Or you'd call me a sinner.
I guess that doesn't leave much.
It's hard in the Spring and the Fall.
I suppose there's no good time to do it
So, just don't die at all!

Druthers

I druther walk along a bubbling, babbling brook
And watch the water rushing o'er the rocks
Than be on an ocean liner on the high seas
Speedily heading for the docks.

I druther indulge in frequent snacks
Than a full-out, gourmet meal,
My tastes are more into snack-food—
Tortilla chips and cheese—now that's a good deal!

I druther listen to a sweet folk song around a campfire
Than enjoy the most poignant love song in my den.
Singing about the Lord or just happy songs,
Is really fun and romantic—do you ken?

I druther have a room that's most eclectic
Filled with pieces that mean more to me,
Than Duncan Fyfe or Louis XIV,
Or even Early American, notably.

But, above all, my druthers are quite simple:
Deep moments with God give my life its zing!
I druther be in His presence—
More than anything!

Eenie, Meenie, Miney and Moe

Eenie, Meenie, Miney and Moe,
Went out on the river, a boat to row.
They really had no plans, nowhere to go,
I've been looking all day for them, you know.

I don't think they'd encounter a big ice floe,
But if they got into trouble, surely someone would tow.
I'm missing those four brothers so.
Where in the world do you think they would go?

They might, per chance, row to Buffalo,
But that would not be very apropos.
And they might, conceivably, go visit Joe.
But I heard he has a big field to mow.

Maybe Melvin—but then again, no.
I waited and wondered and looked high and low,
And, at long last I saw them:
Eenie, Meenie, Miney….but no Moe!

Extolling DVDs

I like the gleam of the sun on the cases,
On the covers of my DVDs.
Oh, I know, no one collects them anymore.
There's so many other options that one sees.

I love the sense of control I have,
I watch them when and where and how;
I simply like collecting them and
Knowing I could view one now.

So many genres represented
But no horror, that's a fact.
Mostly romance and crime shows
I admire the way they act.

Not the heinous crimes, of course,
Explicit sex just turns me off.
I love the back-story in the plot,
So diverse—a kid, a princess, a toff.

I enjoy these covers shown on my shelf,
I watch them, inventory, alphabetize, rearrange.
I've been known to give a few away—
At the very least, some we will exchange.

DVDs may go the way of the eight-track
But with those like me it won't be anytime soon.
I don't anticipate their demise in my lifetime.
A new or used DVD is always a boon!

Ice Cubes

There are few things that I like as much
As ice cubes in my drink.
Even if it's simply water,
I love to sip and hear them clink.

Cold and crunchy and satisfying,
A drink's not a drink without ice.
Cubes, or crushed, or in between,
Oh, so refreshing, oh, so nice!

Do you really like drinks without ice?
Can you really enjoy tepid tea?
And ice water isn't ice water without them,
Or, that's the way it seems to me.

Financial Woes

A slight dent in the exchequer,
A hole in my pocket where money should be,
A glitch in my checkbook
A dollar in my savings,
A bunch of people owe money to me.

But am I dismayed? Do I worry or fret?
What's money to me when I have my health?
Not as good as I usta be
Not as bad as it really could be.
All in all, it's more than wealth!

Itch

In the middle of your back
Did you ever have an itch,
Precisely at the spot
Where your too-short arm can't reach?

Did you ever have a cast
On your leg or arm or ankle?
Then the itch began
And your nerves began to rankle.

Perhaps one day your skin does itch,
It's inside, you just can't touch it.
Sometimes a cream is helpful;
You scratch—you just can't help it.

What is it with an itch?
You know you shouldn't scratch
But you just can't seem to stop
Until you've made a sore patch!

An itch is such an irritant!
Why, I just cannot explain!
I'd rather have a sore than itch—
They both produce much pain.

Good Old Days

I received an email from a friend today
Celebrating things from the past.
It was a test about the "Good Old Days",
Testing to see if my memories last.

It was humorous, and somewhat nostalgic
A blast from the past, as it were,
But I have to say most of those "Good Old Days",
Are nothing more than a blur.

Whoever called them the "Good Old Days",
Was trying to pretend that they liked them.
Who wants to go back to those old times
When even thinking back may be a problem?

Who needs poodle skirts and "beehive" hair-dos,
Ice boxes and jalopies and washers with wringers?
Did you really love the "party-lines" or still prefer your "cell"?
Don't you just love "texting" with your nimble little fingers?

Be nostalgic for those "Good old days", if you will,
But admit you love today's advantages.
Personally, I like instant oatmeal and instant potatoes
And I certainly prefer modern appliances.

Lil Darlin'

Pour me another cup of coffee, Darlin',
And fry up another slab of bacon.
Two or three eggs would go good, too,
My empty ol' belly's just achin'!

Stir up the stove while you're at it,
And put another log on the fire.
If you can't keep up, Lil Sweetheart,
I might have to take someone to hire.

I just can't seem to stir these ol' bones
In the cold or the snow or the rain.
Y'all just have to do them outside chores,
My body's in too much pain.

Oh, do I have another clean shirt?
Maybe the fancy one with the stars.
My buddies are comin' to fetch me;
We're gonna hit a few bars.

Hon, hand me the mornin' paper,
I'd like to read it, if you please.
And pick up that piece of paper for me,
You may have to get on your knees.

What's the matter, Lil Darlin'?
Your face ain't smilin' no more.
You see how much I need you—
Why are you walkin' out the door?

Sad Saga of Smurfy

He was a cross between a little blue Smurf,
And Winnie the Pooh.
Just three feet tall and a little chubby,
He loved to do the things that Smurfies do.

As to his colors, he was in between;
He wasn't blue and he wasn't green,
But, indignantly he'd tell you,
"I'm a lovely aquamarine!"

Smurfy liked to play and laugh and jump,
But, most of all, he loved to eat.
Oh, not onions or Brussel sprouts, you know—
What he really loved was anything sweet.

He had a craving for Mrs. MacDougal's pies,
And Gramma Petrosky's double-chocolate cake.
He wouldn't turn down candy or ice cream or tarts.
Offer him anything with sugar and that he'd take,

One day his mama served beans, ham and salad.
He was a good boy, and ate them all so dutifully.
He waited for dessert but the dessert didn't come.
He held back his tears quite beautifully.

Aunt Polly came to visit that evening.
She surprised him with a sweet that was green.
It was a tinted seafoam candy she made just for him
"It matches, you see, 'cause you're aquamarine!"

Well, Smurfy was happy as happy could be.
He loved his aunt and desserts and surprises.
So, he hugged Aunt Polly, and they all hugged him,
And went to bed blissfully, one surmises!

Sad Saga of Smurfy (cont'd)

Well, it came to pass, as it sometimes does,
That he was in for a rude awakening!
They said he'd get sick if he didn't lose weight
So, there would not be so much sweet-making.

Needless to say, he was more than distraught,
He thought he would die, this poor little boy.
No more of the delicious treats he once sought,
His life, he believed, was devoid of joy!

"Oh, my, no more pie! No more candy or soda!"
He must have cried for days, even wailed.
He was really upset when they told him this
And he realized just what all this "diet" entailed!

The saddest, unhappiest, woebegone boy he was
To think that his beloved sweet treats would be gone.
He couldn't imagine how he'd last the day,
Having to suffice on vegetables alone.

"Now, it's not that bad," his Papa consoled him.
"You'll be surprised how good things can taste
When not covered with sugar or honey.
And you'll learn to eat slowly, not gobble in haste."

To say the least, Smurfy had reservations.
But, maybe, he'd start with sweet potato pie;
That tasted good, and he already liked that,
So, perhaps, there were other things he might try.

To make a very, very long story short,
Smurfy finally learned about a balanced diet,
And even, later, added a sweet or two.
So, all in all, he was glad he'd tried it.

Sad Saga of Smurfy (cont'd)

(If there's a subliminal message somewhere
I have yet to comprehend or heed it!
I blithely go on my merry way in life
Not really obeying, although I need it!)

The Line

Baby, you're the world to me
And that ain't just whistlin' Dixie.
I love your mind and your personality,
But I love your body, mostly.
Is that too risqué of me?
I think you knew that already.

I'd like to get together with you
And see what we two can do.
Maybe we can toss back a few
And see if there is really anything new
That may be done with just us two.
Maybe something we can renew.

Okay, forget it! Be that way!
But I'll call back another day.
Don't think that you can get away,
Because I mean everything I say,
You're just playing hard-to-get today.
Oh, well, if you're married, what can I say?

Little Old Lady

The little old lady is sitting on her porch,
Lounging in her rocking chair, dozing in the sun;
Not thinking of much of anything,
Not even people passing, one by one.

She sits out on her porch each day
In almost any kind of weather
Not rain, of course but early and late
Even though she sometimes wears a sweater.

You may always tell her activities
If you would care to observe,
(Almost like on a "Facebook page")
Her movements seldom swerve.

She looks so sweet and peaceful,
Like she could sit 'til day is done.
I wish we all could have such peace
But I could wish for her some fun.

Little old lady, reclining in her chair
Half asleep and half awake, relaxed.
The sun feels good upon her head,
She is not stressed nor is she taxed.

Basking in the precious rays,
Frittering away the fleeting days,
Oh, say can you see—
That little old lady is me!

Luck

I've heard the quip, "without bad luck you'd have no luck."
I'm beginning to think it may be true in your case.
Except, you know, I don't hold with any kind of luck,
So, those are thoughts you should erase.

I don't pretend to know what God has in store,
But I know you're in the loving hands of Jesus.
It's hard at times to remember that,
Or even that He always sees us.

But somewhere down the road a piece
When things are looking up again,
I know you'll look back and think to yourself,
"Yes, I remember when

I thought I couldn't take any more,
I thought it must surely be the end;
But here I am on the other side,
And really on the mend!"

Misunderstanding

Raymond McCarthy MacGillicuddy Paul
Met with his buddy one day at the Mall.
Said Ray to his friend, "You really have gall
To presume to give my girlfriend a call!
She told me you asked her to go to the ball,
And that you thought she was awfully tall!
What made you say that to my baby doll?
You had no right, George, no right at all!"

So, Georgie Petrosky Adonovich McCall
Answered, "You don't have the right of it at all.
She telephoned me to ask for a shawl.
She said that my sister had made hers too small
And she needed one larger for her sister's doll.
She knew we were friends, and told you she'd call,
Because she needed it way before Fall
To give to her sister who now lives in Ft. Hall."

Raymond said, "Georgie, that still isn't all.
You shouldn't have asked her to go the ball.
Now on our friendship there is a pall.
And I think I shall have to punch you into the wall."
But George, who really wasn't brave or so tall
Made short work of leaving that very same Mall.
He did not want a fight ('cause he was really small)
All over a girl and a shawl for a doll!

Mama was a Flapper

Mama, in her hey-day in the "Roaring Twenties";
You might say she was a "flippin' Flapper".
But not the stereotype "Great Gatsby" woman,
Just a lady, smart and mod and dapper.

They were just independent young ladies,
Intent on enjoyment and seeking their way,
Flouting conventional behavior
An anomaly in their day.

Short skirts, bobbed hair, flagrant actions
Boasting vivid costumes, bracelets and beads,
A "new woman", "liberated" but still lady-like,
Intelligent, resourceful, a very new breed.

Most were happy, gay, all-in-all, enchanting.
Fashionable young ladies, experimenting with life,
Their "rebellion" was only lasting
Until they traded it to be a wife.

Mama was a "Flapper", really "high on life"!
Charming, ebullient and pretty;
Seamlessly, she made the transition
To the country from the city.

Mama was a darling—Daddy loved her!
Throughout their long and happy marriage,
In good times and bad, through thick and thin,
Their union no one would disparage.

Mimi and Me

Mimi and me, I had just turned three,
Proud of our bonnets, as proud could be.
Walking along so happily,
Looking around—so much to see!

Walking this way most every day,
Hoping our friends could come out to play,
Or if they couldn't they wouldn't say,
So, we wouldn't have to go back today.

Mimi and I walking with heads held high,
Nodding and smiling at each passer-by,
Mimi and I, with throats quite dry,
Wondering what next we could try.

Planning on trying to get a drink
From that little puddle, or the kitchen sink.
Trying to guess what Mom might think,
But then, again, she might not even blink.

Mimi and I just swinging along,
Once in a while, singing a song,
Not thinking much about right or wrong,
Big or small or short or long.

Mimi and me strolling down the street,
Best of friends, going out to eat;
Skipping jauntily on our own little feet,
Just the two of us—life is so sweet!

Mimi and Me (cont'd)

A toddler and her dolly, promenading merrily,
Smiling and happy as happy can be!
Walking and talking, whispering quietly;
We are the very best of friends, Mimi and me.

You Lie, Mr. Sky

You lie, Mr. Sky,
You said you would rain, but you lied.
You even spit moisture at my window pane,
I thought you would really open up again,
But you lie, Mr. Sky!
I had my heart set on dancing in the rain,
It's the greatest way to shower;
But I waited in vain.
You fooled me, you rascal,
You didn't even try.
Maybe on another day
You won't lie, Mr. Sky.

Pesky Conscience

You can't always do what you want to do,
Whispers that little voice inside my head.
Does that mean I can't go skinny-dipping
When I should work—or even go to bed?

You need to set a good example
For all those folks around.
Does that mean I have to eat my veggies
Instead of consuming chocolate by the pound?

That sounds like a much better option
Than eating potatoes and meat.
I've never been so fond of veggies,
If I could choose something sweet.

Does it mean that I can't sit relaxing
In my rocker, reading a good book?
Or must I go to the kitchen instead
And begin to learn to cook?

Do I have to clean and scrub and dust
When I'd so much rather go to the beach?
Must I whip up pork and "chittlins"
When I'd rather just eat a peach?

Oh, it's just not any fun having a conscience
That's always telling me what to do!
I'm grown-up now and past the stage
When I have to always be listening to you!

So, get behind me, Conscience
And cut me a little slack.
If you continue with *that* dialogue
I never *will* come back!

Three Little Angels

Three little angels, sitting on a cloud,
Smiling, happy, singing out loud.
One pushed another right off that cloud,
Which left me to surmise,
It wasn't such a big surprise:
You are now by yourself on that cloud.
Some little angel!

The Trav-Man

There's a boy I know who they call Travis
But sometimes he goes by other names, too.
I guess it might depend on if you're mad at him
Or if, perhaps, he talks back to you!

Most of the time he is pretty well-behaved,
And always loving and giving, extremely.
He's bright and cheerful and happy, too,
I love it went he calls me "Mimi".

But that doesn't begin to explain Travy,
So, I'll just tell you of his nick-name, instead;
That might tell you why I'm so fond of him:
I always call him "punkin-head"!

Limbo

Why is this unwanted feeling of "Limbo"
Plaguing me so much lately?
I don't mean that crazy dance with a pole,
That one cannot perform sedately!

I'm talking about feeling neither good nor bad,
"Neither fish nor fowl", as they say.
I mean, that sense of tenterhooks
That seems to pervade my day.

I am not up, nor am I really down.
I am neither sad nor blue nor happy.
If there is such a feeling, I feel "pleasant".
Perhaps I just need some therapy?

Morning

I don't hit the ground running anymore,
I ease into the day with my morning routine:
Morning ablutions, meds and meditation,
All the things that start a day, you know what I mean.

I have just recently come to this conclusion:
There's just something wrong with a day
That begins with getting up!
In my bed I'd rather stay.

Scales

I think my scales are mocking me.
They smile within and laugh at me.
They know that I can barely see
So, they falsify the facts, you see.

It's plain for anyone to see
That no one gains as much as me
Nor plunges the next day so quickly:
My scales are certainly mocking me.

They take my hopes unerringly
And plummet them despairingly;
I'm disgruntled, can't you see?
My scales are actually mocking me.

Why can't they just stay on one key;
Why can't I appreciate what the numbers be?
Instead I argue helplessly,
"This isn't what they ought to be!"

Why do they keep me in a quandary,
Wondering on which day I'll see
The numbers where they ought to be?
My scales are truly mocking me.

Retail Therapy

Retail therapy is really nothing new,
You might say I'm a "shopaholic", too;
It's bad when periodically my credit I renew.
And even worse when my bills are due.

Retail therapy is the best prescription to stop feeling blue.
I sometime shop for dresses, perhaps another shoe,
I'm addicted to DVDs and books that are new.
More often I just look around for a tchotchke or two.

Sometimes I gaze in shop windows, choices to renew;
There's even a little candy store down on the Avenue,
I find my feet unerringly, inevitably drawn to.
Or I take time for a frothy latte or a foamy brew.

Psychologists, recommend this more—
It's certainly nothing new:
Retail therapy will do the trick,
Even after we say, "Dr. Who?"

Seriously Stoo-ped!

You put your wet finger into an electric outlet—
You try to lick an icy pole—
You bite off more than you can chew—
By yourself dig an enormous hole—
Seriously stoo-ped!

Three things at a time you think you can do—
You lift more than you can possibly carry—
You hang on to someone when they are gone—
Or more than one you want to marry—

So many things you've tried and failed
So many more you think you can do.
Has history and logic taught you nothing?
Would you just quit trying if you only knew?
Or continue to be… Seriously Stoo-ped?

Slurp

Soup is better when you slurp;
This is not the time for manners.
Succumb to your inalienable right to slurp,
Then, if it was good, you burp.

Darning

Do I know how to darn, you ask?
I've darned many a sock in my day.
I won't say I liked it, 'cause I didn't.
At this late date, all I can say is
Darn, darn, darn!

Whatever

The laziest word in the dictionary is "whatever".
It's for people who don't want to think.
The easiest answer to make is "whatever",
And it's done without even a blink.

We could say "yes" or "I'll think about it",
Or we could even say "no";
Whatever gets us off the hook
To reply without making a foe.

We're so busy pleasing people
We seldom have a real thought of our own.
So, we answer, "whatever" without thinking,
That way our cover's not blown.

Thereby, we aren't responsible for a little white lie
Because we've not really made a decision.
We stay on the shelf with "wishy" and "washy",
Not making a conscious choice is our mission.

Wash Day

I still remember "wash day"
The sights, the smells, the ambience
As if it were yesterday:
The whirr of the old wringer-washer,
The heat and the steam and the spray.
The smell of the fresh-air-dried clothes,
The sweet-scented sheets, what can I say?
The scent of soup cooking on the stove
Would for the home-coming student convey
That feeling of "home", of security,
And many memories along the way.
But getting your hand caught in the wringer—
I still will choose "today"!

Tiny Tea Cup

There was a tiny tea cup
As pretty as could be,
With posies painted on it
Out of which we drank our tea.

This tiny little tea cup
Was there for friend or foe.
To solidify a friendship
Or remove a mighty woe.

I loved this tiny tea cup
And used it every day.
And then it broke!
I'm holding tears at bay!

Ode to an Outhouse

I'm probably one of the few remaining ones
That still remember that tiny hut in the back yard;
Not only that, but remember it fondly!
I really enjoyed it, tho' times may have been hard.

It was my private get-away,
A place I could really be alone;
I could sing out loud and contemplate—
The only place I was truly on my own.

If, perchance, you had a two-holer,
You might share it with a very good friend,
But, just generally speaking,
That's not something I'd recommend.

Modern bathrooms are certainly more convenient,
With their nice, white porcelain sinks;
And, I admit, I enjoy the tubs and showers—
But, really, the acoustics stink!

At Loose Ends

My project is complete, my book is done.
I feel so at loose ends, like a balloon let loose.
I might fizzle and sputter if popped!
Then I feel like my neck's in a noose.
I am tied up in knots, wondering where
I am going and what I should do.
Why am I procrastinating? Why so blue?
I've accomplished what I set out to do.
Now I've reached the second-guessing stage
Why did I do just that?
Why did I do it that way?
Could I have made some improvements?
Why did I send it, anyway!
I've said it before, I'll just say it again:
It is what it is what it is!
It's all in God's hands now,
And what better hands than His?

SECTION II

OCCASIONS

Birthday

Easter

Christmas

Thanksgiving

2017

Mean what you say, and say what you mean
Is my motto for two-thousand-seventeen.
I'm tired of everyone, including myself,
Who speaks with fork-ed tongue, or so it seems.
The Bible says, let your aye be aye
Your nay be nay—on that I lean.
To some that may seem a bit extreme,
To achieve that awesome end I'm very keen.

2019

I have a vision for 2019
It's not much different from other years,
Just, perhaps, less time to achieve it.
A lot more joys, sometimes more tears
But all in all, at the end of the year
There will be a lot less fears!
But wanting more is almost obscene.
Let's make a pact to be joyful in 20-19.

2020

2020 is a new year and a brand-new beginning
It will be whatever you and God will make of it.
It may be the turning point for that which you have prayed,
It could be finally finding out where in His plan you fit.

A new year is a pristine slate to write upon;
It always holds so many possibilities;
Anything can happen, and it will!
You must be ready to embrace it to the best of your abilities.

85

This year I painted a Birthday Painting:
I depicted an eagle, soaring in the sky,
Psalm 103 I quoted, about His benefits—
I'm renewed like the eagle, flying high.

Also, in Isaiah— 40:31, to be precise:
I will be as the eagle—I can almost hear it cry—
"You are the redeemed of the Lord!
And He will always satisfy!"

So now I've reached the unheard-of age
I never dreamed I would arrive at—85.
Perhaps the last year of my life on earth?
I can only conjecture—will I be alive

When another year rolls around,
Or in Heaven will I finally arrive?
But while I am here I'll work for Him;
He knows that's for what I'll strive.

Seventy-Two and Holding

Happy Birthday to me, Happy Birthday to me!
Even turning seventy-two is a big deal to me.
Imagine what I'll feel like when turning seventy-three!

My poor old ankle acts up once in a while,
My feet ain't as good as they used to be;
I feel on this day that I sure ain't no chile
My knees, hips and back they ain't dancey.

Seventy-Two and Holding (cont'd)

My nose ain't so bad, as noses go,
But it now has some scars I ain't showin',
My mouth still is turnin' up like a bow,
And my mind is definitely still growin'.

The old eyes need these panes to hide behind,
And even then, they just don't do night;
But still I can read and drive up a storm,
And as long as I can, I'm all right!

At seventy-two I'm still sharp as a tack,
Though the point on the tack's a bit blunted;
My memories are keen and I know quite a bit
About a lot—'cause I've hunted.

Yep, my get up and go has got up and went,
And my "live-in" is old Arthur Itus;
But most of the time we don't fight too much,
He's much better than old Penn D'Citis!

I have 4 other friends in whom I delight:
Ben and Jerry and Baskin and Robbin;
I can't indulge with them too many times
As they're makin' me look like Old Dobbin.

I feel great and I'm happy and singing a song
As I continue completing my task;
I'm old but I'm free and still young in the Lord—
In that I will always bask.

Happy Birthday to me, Happy Birthday to me!
I'm happily going along merrily.
Join me in singing and being all we can be
To God and each other, indefinitely!

Fourscore

I have something in common with the "Gettysburg Address":
I can finally claim the word "Fourscore".
It's been so long and yet so short,
It's been so little and yet so "more".

When I was young, fifty seemed so old.
It wasn't an age I thought I'd ever achieve;
But time marches on and so do birthdays
And when 60 arrived I was somewhat relieved.

After that it was all a blur:
70' and 80's were incomprehensible!
"I'll never get that old," I thought.
My arguments were indefensible.

Time and tide wait for no man.
Before I blinked twice—or maybe it was more—
I arrived at that which I once deemed impossible:
That previously unheard of . . ."Fourscore";
And God alone can tell if I'll get to 81 or more!

My Birthday

On the eve of another birthday
I pause and simply contemplate
My life and its ramifications,
Wondering if the past I'd duplicate?
    Some things yes, some no.

But everything in all my life
Makes me who I am today;
The things that I did and every thought,
All the good, the bad and shades of gray.
    It's all a part of me.

Wrapping up a long, long life
Is not an easy feat, it's true;
One cannot encapsulate
Such a span with words so few.
    It is foolish to even try.

Birthdays have always been special to me
I'm the greatest "celebrator", by far!
I really know how to do birthdays—
One year I even bought myself a new car!
    Nothing to show for that now.

My Birthday (cont'd)

This year I have topped them all off:
I have had my first book published.
My "baby was born" late in July,
But I'm not close to being finished.
    Maybe next birthday she'll have a sibling.

In spite of the things that are wrong with me
I am a very happy participant in life.
I wouldn't know how to cope with "all good",
One must inevitably have some strife.
    But, this much?

I'm jesting, of course, being facetious;
I don't like to dwell on the negative.
I strive to be healthy, happy and whole—
Now I'm being alliterative.
    The poet within me?

All in all, I thank You, Lord,
For giving me this wondrous day,
And week, and month and year
In which to live and laugh and say
    I love You, Jesus!

1975

You wrote me on Your heart, Lord,
Before I was even born.
You guided all my footsteps
When I was happy or forlorn.

I had a happy childhood
But I wasn't really born 'til 1975.
My whole life led up to that,
The day I finally became alive.

I don't know why I waited so long
Or if You were the One Who was waiting
For me to realize what I was missing;
To You my life I'd be dedicating.

In spite of my wrong turns and wrong doings,
You guided and guarded me throughout my life.
I finally realized them for what they were—
My sins were running rife.

Oh, I know that I'm not perfect now,
I doubt I am even close.
You know that I am trying, somehow,
And my failings I'm able to diagnose.

Perfection is only in You, Lord,
But now I know that I can strive
To be the person You told me I could be
Back in 1975!

Thanksgiving Reverie

What am I thankful for this year?
Oh, so many, many blessings!
I can't even put it all down on paper
It's not just the turkey and dressing.

My family, of course, and loved ones
And those with whom I'm dining,
And the special memories I am sharing today
Instead of being in bed, reclining.

I loved my life, for the most part
And *those* parts are forgotten, dismissed;
I am grateful for "selective memory",
Ignoring those I have kissed!

For my gifts of poetry and painting
Tho' they may not please anyone else—
What would I have done without them?
I have always needed goals for myself.

And for all my family—quite a crew!
Some have stayed close, some have not,
But I rejoice in their love all the same,
And exult in the bonds we have wrought.

I'm grateful for my Salvation and walk with the Lord,
And that all my family, as far as I know,
Have accepted the Truth, as well
And are currently walking in the Word.

Most Beautiful Dawn

The most beautiful dawn that ever was,
The most glorious Morn that ever could be,
The most magnificent Occurrence in history,
The most unbelievable Occasion for you and me
And for one and all, through the ages;
For us and all our progeny:
Resurrection Morning! Alleluia!

He Is Risen

He is risen! He is risen, indeed!
Not just Easter Sunday, but today;
He is here for each of us, if we but heed;
He is ever here in every way.

He was not risen, in the past tense,
Not just *was* risen but *is* risen, indeed!
In every manner that we can and cannot sense.
Jesus is risen, He is risen indeed!

Have you experienced that truth?
Do you know that you know that you know?
If you love Him, will you be as Ruth
And say, "Whither Thou goest I will go"?

Even if you don't, He s risen, indeed!

Resurrection Day

Easter isn't bunnies
Or colored Easter eggs—
It's Jesus.
Easter isn't pageants
Or marvelous cantatas—
It's Jesus.

He came to earth
For such a time as this;
He came, He died, He rose again
So, all of us might live
In the glorious certainty
Of Resurrection Day.

He lived for us
He died for us
He was resurrected to prove
That He truly is the Messiah.

Accept His sacrifice again.
Rededicate yourself to Him
On Resurrection Day.......and always.

Christmas Season

It's another Christmas Season,
Another Christmas night.
Parties to be planning,
Gifts furtively pushed out of sight.
It may be different this year,
But it still will be all right.

The cherished Christmas ornaments
Are once again in place,
The colored lights, the holly,
But missing is the frenzied pace.
No more pushing, prodding, scheming,
No more Christmas-time rat-race.

Everything is changing,
No more status quo.
Yes, every year is different,
But that is how we grow.
One just rolls with the punches,
It's a new year, don't you know?

We must embrace the new time,
Traditions are sometimes made to be broken.
But the tradition of love and of family
Is always much more than a token
Of all we remember and care for
In all the sweet words we have spoken.

As families increase and decrease
It's the ebb and flow of life;
We enjoy the one time all year
That seems to be free of strife;
The warmth between siblings and offspring,
And even estranged husband and wife.

Christmas Season (cont'd)

It's yet another Christmas Season,
And the world seems to be so right.
Enmity is pushed aside for a time
And we forget the woes and plight,
When we concentrate on the Season
And that glorious Christmas Night.

Oh, the beautiful Christmas Season,
Ever-changing yet somehow the same;
If we can't feel the wonder of Christmas
We have only ourselves to blame.
It's always different, yes that's true,
But still when Jesus came!

Celebrate Christmas

I celebrate Christmas because it's all about Him.
I enjoy the gleaming lights
To remind me He is the Light of the World.
I hang a wreath because He is
The unbroken circle of life,
The Alpha and Omega, beginning and the end.
He is Joy, so I am joyful;
He is Peace, so I am peaceful;
If it is not, for you, then it is because
You are not allowing it to be.
You are not focusing on Jesus.

Meaning of Christmas

It's really hard to find the words
To say what Christmas means to me
It encompasses so very, very much
I can't convey everything it means to me.

Right, or wrong, I truly love the sparkle and glitter,
I enjoy the color, the presents, and all the lights!
I even like the shopping frenzy and the angst
The happy faces on all the little sprites!

I love the Christmas music every year,
The Christmas songs, both old and new
I play and sing them from October
Even belting out that Christmas so Blue!

But I really know what Christmas is all about
And I revere the holidays for His sake.
It's not just another Birthday Party,
For all the happy fuss we make!

I know from where my Salvation comes,
I realize it started with that Precious Baby
I love the beautiful Nativity scenes
On mantels, on window sills, maybe.

The candlelight service is always so special
A time to calm down and reflect on His birth
We are gathering with family,
And people all over the earth!

Yes, I love the secular ambience of Christmas,
I love everything that makes it a special season.
Most of all, of course, I love Jesus—
He's still the most important part—the Reason!

Christmas Is a Promise

Christmas is a promise coming true
Of everything you've dreamed of, longed for, hoped for;
A nebulous, intangible, can't-put-your-finger-on-it
Yearning desire for something more;
And if I should happen to shed a wee tear
At the height of the Christmas festivities,
It's because I'm just a sentimental fool
And always will be, if you please!

To a Christmas Crèche

Not politically correct, I hear,
To see a Christmas Crèche appear,
But its beauty makes one shed a tear.
It may be plain or colored brightly,
Antique or modern or something sprightly,
But always positioned just so rightly.
I never take a Christmas crèche lightly!

Mistletoe

From lowly to lovely this parasite has come
To symbolize the joy and happiness of kissing.
While once it meant something unsavory,
That definition is, gladly, missing.

So, pucker up, for tradition's sake,
If not because you want him to kiss you.
One never knows when a "traditional" act
Will turn into another "I do."

Mary's Heart

I'm so very, very tired tonight,
And we could not find a bed.
I'm weary of the traveling
But there's no place to lay my head.

And then my wondrous baby came—
That long-awaited birth!
I know that He was also anticipated
By every soul on earth!

I feel so very "all-grown-up"
And yet not much more than a child.
I know not why God has blessed me so
With this awesome, precious child!

I feel exceedingly inadequate
To be the mother of His Son—
And how must my dear Joseph feel
After all is said and done?

We know what God has said to do,
We follow as He leads us,
To create this "Holy Family"
And care for Baby Jesus.

The cattle and the oxen all
Are hovering o'er this manger
In which we'll place our Infant Son
To keep Him from cold and danger.

He nestles into fragrant straw
And makes little baby mews.
Unaware that all the angels
Are heralding the Great News.

Mary's Heart (cont'd)

Christ the Lord is born this night:
The world will never be the same.
For this moment I was born,
For this time in history Jesus came.

I close my eyes and thank my God;
I cuddle Him closely to my breast.
But it is only the beginning;
There is no time for rest.

He must fulfill His destiny,
And I'll be a mother to Him,
While fulfilling that of my own—
It's God's edict, not His whim.

One day my heart will break in two
As His destiny encroaches.
I must watch my Son be killed
As the enemy approaches.

But God will be with me through it all
And grant me strength and blessing.
I'll be the mother God intended,
Not easily, I'm confessing.

He may be your Messiah
But he's so much more to me:
My baby boy, my son, my love,
My precious child He'll always be.

But this night I will not think of this;
I'll simply be content
To hold my Child and love Him,
And praise the Father, so benevolent!

What I Want for Christmas

What do I want for Christmas?
'Tis probably what everybody wishes:
Peace on earth must head the list,
But I'm wise enough to know that won't be
Until the Lord returns again,
And takes with Him His children.
For now, I wish for happiness
For those who do not feel it,
I wish for food and clothing warm
For all the poor and homeless folks
I wish, too, that I could help
In my small way, to make this happen.
I wish the desires of the hearts
Of all deserving people.
I pray for the peace of God for my family.
I wish to make a difference
In the lives of those I touch.
That the world might be a better place
For once having me in it.
You know what I wish, it goes without saying:
That everyone in the world will know the Lord!

At Christmas Time

Do I have in me another Christmas Rhyme?
Inspirational, funny, not many sublime.
I write often of this most joyful time,
Even now, when I'm well past my prime.
I reach for more words to show that I'm
Wanting to say it in words—I'm not into mime.
I'll just say I'm the happiest at Christmas Time!

Know Jesus

Another Christmas season is upon us.
I must have lived "a million of 'em" by now.
Good ones, bad ones, happy and sad ones
I can't remember all of 'em, anyhow.

But there a few I will never forget,
No matter how old I ever become.
Strangely, I don't recall the people or gifts,
Or even the things that day that I've done.

It's more the overall emotional high
That permeates my being.
The feelings that I remember,
More than that which I was seeking.

I pray at the start of each Season
For peace and joy and happiness.
But above all that, the preeminent prayer:
I wish for everyone to know Jesus!

Kiss the face of Jesus

I love the painting where Mary kisses
The Face of Jesus, the Babe,
I can't even imagine that marvelous feeling.
I can't wait until that fabulous day
I can kiss the face of Jesus, the man.

My Christmas

The glowing star atop the shiny tree,
The glittering lights and the ornaments you see,
    Are not my Christmas.

The food, the friends, the frolicking in the snow,
The joyous camaraderie everywhere you go,
    Are not my Christmas.

All the decorations, lovely as they are,
From the tiniest angel to the shiniest star,
    These are not my Christmas.

There are packages galore underneath the branches,
The least amount of movement causes avalanches.
    That is not my Christmas.

Then melodies of carolers upon a Christmas Eve,
So marvelous these songs, one *cannot* grieve.
    But these are not my Christmas.

Such wonderful memories of Christmases past,
And the joy and the peace and the love that will last,
    But still, that's not my Christmas,

Even the Manger Scenes—Holy Mary, meek and mild,
Manly Joseph and the precious Infant Child—
    Now it's closer to my Christmas,

Without any of the things above,
Even without family or friends, or even love,
I would still have Christmas.
    For Christmas is Jesus
    And Jesus is my Christmas

Post-Holiday Let-Down

After Christmas, Thanksgiving or Birthday
Comes the inevitable downward spin;
No matter that you try to stave it off,
It happens—you just can't win.
Maybe it's the frenetic hustle and bustle,
The planning, the plotting, the anticipation
Engendered by a happy coming event,
Or all the purchases and preparation.
Holidays are special occasions
To everyone, if you're truthful;
Youngster or oldster it's still the same,
Even if you're no longer youthful

But after it's over and the holiday's passed,
There's no more planning and everything's done,
It may have been all you wanted it to be
But it's just too much for some.
You can't do anything about it—
The weariness is settling in.
Yes, it's mental, but it's physical, too;
A profound lethargy seems to begin;
So overwhelming are the symptoms
If you didn't know better you'd think you were ill:
The blues, the blahs, whatever you call it,
You think it won't pass—but it will!

I Survived Covid-19

Is this an "occasion" to write about?
Well, it's something we'll not soon forget.
It's not easy to conjecture the ramifications,
And I know everyone is upset.

I remember the hurricanes in Florida,
And the devastation some of them did.
But I also saw firsthand, at the end of one,
How the greed was never hid:

We all thought it fun to wear T-shirts
Sporting "I survived Hurricane Honey"!
Well, that wasn't its name, but it's the same,
You'll admit, someone made money!

Will we look back on all this, wear a T-shirt
That states, "I survived Covid-19"?
Is it cynical to say I can anticipate that day,
Or, is this all, perhaps, a bad dream?

I admire the dedicated workers
Who are helping us all through this scourge.
I pray for the ill and families of the deceased.
But, at times, I indulge this cynical urge!

We've all survived much in our lifetimes.
I am sure that one day this will all be behind;
I pray for a better world, like most of us,
But I know that none are deaf, dumb and blind.

I Survived Covid-19 (cont'd)

Believe me I'm not making light of the threat
That is touching our world and our nation;
Just reserving the right, to survive this plight,
And rejoice, at the end, with a grand celebration!

Someday soon, I hope, this scare will have abated
And the survivors will emerge on the other side.
We will be better, somehow, for the scare we had,
Not rejoicing in this major roller-coaster ride!

Let's vow to all be the best we can be
And remember the heartache involved.
We may be a bit cynical, but we're optimists, too.
If we all do our best......problem solved!

SECTION III

GOD'S
WORLD

Nature

His Creation

Cloudy Sunset

Silvered pewter clouds above a polished pewter sea,
But, lo, a glint of gold there to the west!
Putty-colored sand amid the rivulets of water,
Tinted lightly where the sun caressed.

Breezes moving swiftly in the evening's waning light,
Scuttling waves and clouds before their paths;
Rippling steel gray waves dappled by the gold,
Seabirds tiptoe lightly down for their nocturnal baths.

The undulating seashore of beige and taupe and tan
Seems to be anticipating night.
The heavens wait with bated breath the climax of the day
When the golden sun extinguishes its light.

Even in a cloudy sky the glory of the sunset
Manifests itself in full array;
As with one final burst of splendor the sun-flame is extinguished
And dusky evening settles down to stay.

Glorious Sunrise

My heart exults in Your glorious sunrise,
My senses reel in Your wondrous day;
My emotions soar beholding Your skies,
I must sing of the beauty of Your ways.

I wonder why early man didn't know it was You
That created this marvelous orb called the sun?
The glory, the majesty, the beauty of it should
Be evidence that You were the One.

Perfect Seashell

A walk along the seashore
May be good for more than that—
A timely lesson it may teach.

If you really listen to the
Soothing voices of the waves
A simple message they will preach.

Running, scurrying, seeking, sometimes finding,
Looking for that special seashell on the beach;
Bending, stooping, peering, grabbing for that one
There—just out of reach.

Then, stop, lay supine upon the shore—relax!
Contemplate the beauty of the seagull tracks,
Stretch out upon the warm, inviting sand,
Then open up your eyes—there by your hand—
That tiny, elusive, lovely, perfect shell!

Nature

Nature's very hard to beat,
There's nothing really any better.
God's world is so spectacular
In any kind of weather.

I'm not really an "animal lover",
And bugs I've never been fond of,
But there's no gainsaying, the Master's Plan
Is something one must love.

The world around is fabulous,
One must agree, be it country or city,
At the very least, we must admit,
His world, it sure is pretty!

Winter Sun

Basking in the winter sun,
Shining through my window;
Sitting in my comfy chair,
Relaxed and pensive and happy.
Whoever built this house, or had it built
Must have sat in this very same spot
To know just where the sun would come in
On a winter afternoon….Thank you.
It may be eighteen degrees outside
But inside it's sunny and cozy
It doesn't take much to make me happy—
To make me feel my world is rosy!

Deep Blue World

There's a strange unearthly music
To the silence of the sea:
Diving down beneath the waters,
Deep as any man can be.

Colors only once before encountered
In the corners of your mind;
Things you've never once imagined
In that deep blue world you'll find

Coral fingers, outward reaching,
Grasping for eternity;
Down to basics—living, struggling,
Basis for humanity.

A fish in a fish in a fish in a fish,
Color on color on color on color;
Moving, lurching, seeking, searching,
  Deep
    Deep
      Down.

Country Contemplation

Once I watched twin elks born
At the bottom of my yard!
To witness such a miracle
And praise the Creator wasn't hard.

In the mornings there are turkeys here,
Sometimes six—or ten—or more,
Strutting proudly down my country road.
I wonder if the asphalt makes their feet sore?

Across the way, upon the hill,
The tawny deer do play.
A neighbor feeds them faithfully
Almost every single day.

They feed and gambol playfully,
At times there've been a dozen or more,
Oblivious of people, cars and such;
But lately, there's usually four.

I sometimes see, from my bedroom window,
A pudgy little groundhog,
Foraging avidly in the tall weeds.
At first, I mistook it for a dog.

Of course, there's dogs my neighbors keep,
And birds and cats galore.
I have all the joy of country
Right at my back door!

Computer Gardening

A computer is a handy tool to have, especially for my "dreamery".
I'd focus on the woods across the street
Then try to improve the scenery.
This could take the better part of a day.

I'd zoom in on the underbrush and broken tree limbs—
The first thing on my agenda—to eradicate them all.
A few, of course, for artistic aesthetics,
But I really like a nice, clean landscape, overall.

Then I'd move on to other portions of my yard.
I know what I'd like to add and what to remove.
A computer is easier than yardwork—that's very hard!
But after I am finished, just what would I prove?

That I am better at this than God, my Father?
I know He has it all in His plan and power;
Gardening is really such a time-consuming bother,
But I'll save my computer for another job, another hour.

Dawn

Slowly and surely comes the dawn,
As the sun peeps o'er the hill,
Coming after the night has gone
When everything is still.

To begin the new day with perfection
And steal away the night.
Without suspicion of detection,
That everyone may deem if right.

God's Flowers

I'm sitting in my yard surveying flowers.
Not everyone's in my garden, some are in my mind.
I've viewed so many blossoms all around the world
I cannot possibly name my favorite kind.

There's some I don't even know the name of,
But I so enjoy all the vibrant and vivacious colors!
I "get off" on color—can't explain it—
Even when I can't identify the flowers.

Flowers have a language, I am told.
You'd best be careful which you give to whom!
You could be conveying your love for someone
When all you wanted was to enjoy the bloom!

Appreciation for lovely flowers can't be over-rated;
There's no such thing as too many, too great, too much.
They are most definitely some of God's masterpieces,
Along with trees and sky and such!

I can't write a rhyme for every flower,
They all, like us, fit so nicely in His world.
Big and tall, tiny and small, all the colors
He originated, all fluffed up and curled.

Straight and spikey, great and mighty,
All existing in close harmony,
Almost exuding poignant melody;
The flowers of God's world are such a blessing,
To everything, everyone, every time.

Sparkling Sea-Oats

The sea-oats is not one to blow its own horn,
Its usefulness is legend in coastal parts;
But when the sunlight turns her fronds to feather
It shines and sparkles, touching the hardest of hearts.

Stately Sunflower

Vibrant, majestic, stately sunflower,
Rising tall to peer above the fence,
Surveying a vast kingdom, exercising power
Over other flowers in the gardens dense.

Sweet Daisy

Sweet and pretty, brown or yellow-eyed daisy:
The flower kingdom's favorite ingenue.
You brighten the garden even when the sky is hazy.
So unpretentious against the backdrop of sky-blue.

Stunning Orchid

Stunning orchid, tall and stately,
Pink and white and yellow.
I love each and every one of them
Their presence keeps me mellow.

Hibiscus

I had a friend who greeted his flowers every morning;
He'd emerge from his door and smile and wave.
Just as the glorious day was dawning
He'd call, "Hi, Biscus" and the day would be happy, not grave.

Blossoms

God's blowing a blossom before my window pane,
From the beautiful forsythias close by on the lawn.
Yellow branches waving, like a spirited horse's mane,
And the sky seems to suggest it possibly might rain.

The blossoms are so lovely—I try to capture them in vain.
I couldn't grasp them in my mortal hand,
Nor reproduce them on canvas for posterity,
Nor even write a suitable poem, it drives me insane!

The Lily

The tulip and the lily and chrysanthemum,
Proliferate the country gardens wide.
Orange tiger lilies against the soft gray barn
Never a sight one can deride.

The fragrance of the pink and white ones,
Ever giving off their pungent scent.
Oh, if one could only be a lovely lily
Beauty would follow everywhere one went.

Perfect, Picturesque Pepper

Perfect picturesque, lovely green Pepper;
Perfectly symmetrical, more that nature intended.
    Dangling from the mother plant
    The stalk so gently bends;
Oh, so picture-perfect in a Harvest centerpiece
Or on one's plate, as God intended.

Voluptuous Tomato

Luscious, voluptuous, red, ripe Tomato:
Delicious, delectable, nutritious and more.
Best of the best, the food of the gods,
Always enjoyable to the core.

Vibrant, versatile as a side or main dish,
Fantastic in juices, pastas and sauces,
Main ingredient in casseroles
And in the salads that one tosses.

Vibrant Violets

Vivid African Violets—my favorite indoor plant.
The colors, the textured velvet leaves and flowers
Grow rampant on my sunny window sill
I could simply gaze at them for hours and hours.

Ode to a Fawn

I glimpsed a fawn today and thought:
What a graceful animal God has wrought.
The deer, uninhibited, crossing the road,
Seeking food, as they flee to their abode.
They'd not yet learned to distrust man,
So, blithely, nimbly, onward they ran,
Oh, to be so unrestrained and carefree,
They seem to stop and smile at me.

Butterfly

Flitting, floating, flying butterfly,
One of the loveliest of God's creatures.
 Beautiful to watch
 Not easy to catch,
A certain favorite of Mother Nature's.

All the lovely colors of the rainbow,
As well as black and white for accent.
 I wonder what God meant
 When butterflies He sent
Maybe to give us all a lovely present.

Praying Trees

I so enjoy the view that I'm afforded,
The glorious trees I out my window spy,
Waving happily to the snowy clouds,
Their leafy arms uplifted to the sky,
As if in prayer to their Creator;
I ever smile at them and sigh.
I also offer up my eyes and arms in praise.

Trees

I think that I shall never see—
No, Kilmer already did that, splendidly.
But I can still be in awe of a tree
And how they have affected me.
They stand so tall and so stately,
And often provide their shade for me.
There are those whose fruit I eat gladly
And those of such magnificent beauty
That one must just gaze appreciatively,
Caught up in poignant enormity
Of one of God's blessings, created for me!
No, this poem can never do justice to a tree—
Neither did Kilmer's, if you ask me!

January, a Time for Song

The aftermath of Christmas,
January is a waiting time;
It's rather anticlimactic,
But still can be sublime.
It's cold and rather inclement,
At least, in a northern clime.

In January our thoughts turn to snow,
Even tho' that weather man could be wrong;
At times it's rain, sometimes there's sun,
But always the dark, dark nights are long.
Perk up! There's always a reason for joy,
There's always a reason to sing a song.

It's March

It's March. I saw a fly today,
Does that mean Spring is coming?
Winter has been hard for me
Spring I won't be shunning!

March

"Flustery", blustery month of March,
Right in the middle of cold, dismal days;
Disgusted with Winter, longing for Spring,
Yearning for more marvelous sun rays.

No times of great occasions, or events,
Just before or after all the holidays;
Once every few years there is Easter,
But most of the time that comes with some delays.

But March can be a pleasant time
If one but takes it as it comes;
A sort of "backing up for a running start" time,
Between the snowflakes and the mums.

Don't allow a period of dreariness,
Don't permit yourself to fall into the doldrums.
For what your mind and heart dwells on
Is what your personality eventually becomes.

Only May

Saw a bumble bee today
And it is only May!
I noticed it was big and fat,
What's up with that?

Points of Light

I love to gaze at the sky at night,
God's wondrous points of light,
In a stygian night-sky so bright.
Sometimes the darkness begets fright.

The Sea

Oh, the glory of the rolling sea
Gazing from my deck chair, appreciatively,
Midday sun shining down on me,
One can't but think of Thee.
Writing snippets of poetry,
Extolling the ocean, sometimes smooth and glassy.
But then the waves can roar so violently!

If I had enough faith I could walk to Thee,
Walk on the water, peacefully.
I watch the gulls sweep gracefully
I could see a dolphin, imminently.
I have gotten off-track, in praising the sea,
But every thought and line also rhyme with Thee!

Squirrels

Being a squirrel is a lot less complicated
Than being a human being!
Jump, hop, chatter, clamber up trees,
Grab a nut and run down again!

Maybe look out for a predator or two,
But no love triangles to drive you crazy.
No worry about what you're going to wear
It wouldn't cross your mind to be lazy.

The life of a squirrel seems a happy one,
At least from what I've observed.
They're active and playful and frisky
And, seemingly, never reserved!

Oh, for the life of a bushy-tailed squirrel,
Or a flying squirrel high in a tree,
Freely soaring from limb to limb—
Think how happy that would make me.

Until I encounter the neighbor's Tomcat.
That would not make me happy at all!
I was blithely going about my business
When that darned cat made me fall!

Tribute to the States

Oklahoma, Pennsylvania, New York and New Jersey
And our newest state, Hawaii;
Georgia, Nevada, Kentucky and Tennessee
They're all states I'd like to see.

.

There's Nebraska, Arizona and Kansas;
Delaware, Alabama, Texas and Washington;
Mississippi, Louisiana, Connecticut,
New Hampshire, Michigan, Montana and Oregon.

I've lived in many of the states:
Among my favorites are Virginia and Florida,
I'm sure I would like others, too, if I would try;
North and South Carolina and California.

I *have* lived in Alaska, but I will say no more.
It could be an acquired taste, like, say, Indiana;
Then there are those cold states, Maine, Vermont,
North Dakota, South Dakota, Minnesota.

Some of these I'd like to visit, just to say I've been:
Massachusetts, Illinois, Iowa and Arkansas
Sound great to visit sometime soon,
As does Wyoming, Montana and Utah.

West Virginia is another one I love to travel through,
I've been many times to see Ohio.
Someday I'll see Wisconsin and Missouri,
Colorado, Idaho and New Mexico.

I'm proud that I can remember them all
But I almost overlooked Rhode Island!
I almost always remember the state
Below me, called Maryland.

Pennsylvania

The pearl of the Mid-Atlantic States,
Pennsylvania's beauty is unsurpassed.
The verdant mountains and fruitful valleys
"Penn's Woods" will never be outclassed.

I like the climes in other places,
Some things about them I still recall.
Some may have better Summers or Winters,
But few have such a magnificent Fall.

Pennsylvania has so much to be said of it,
My faltering fingers just can't do it justice.
Its beauty, its history, so many things I could list here,
But, I need to go on, forthwith.

The best that Pennsylvania has to offer
Isn't something you read or say or see,
It's so important, you will agree—
I am happy here with my family!

Blooming Trees

The flowering trees in bloom are magnificent to behold!
Dogwood, Forsythia, Oleander, Magnolia, and the fruit trees,
Each with their vivid color and fragrant beauty
Their splendor and majesty bring me to my knees!

Awe-inspiring, to say the very least, they take your breath away.
They are impressive in their finery, a miracle in motion,
When the lively winds blow through their branches
They're reminiscent of the undulating ocean.

Jaunty Jacaranda

My favorite tree in all the world is the Jaunty Jacaranda!
Its vivid purple blossoms fill the eyes and soul.
Just strolling underneath one makes a heart feel gay,
Makes one's mind and body once again feel whole!

There's something so spectacular about this purple tree,
Even when the blooms are gone their lacy leaves are lovely.
The first time that I saw one, I was instantly enchanted,
As I observed the breeze blow the blooms so awesomely!

Unending Scene

The stately tree towering over me
Is a wondrous sight to see;
From the flowering bush I get a rush,
A thrill from the warbling thrush.
The panorama of green on green
Is a changing, unending scene.
I never tire of this selection!
Oh, to be surrounded endlessly
By such amazing perfection!

Brown-Eyed Susan

Some say they have black eyes,
But my mom maintained the flower's eye was brown.
My Daddy always picked them for her—
They were her favorite, and her eyes were brown.

Pretty Little Plants

Pretty little plants on my window sill
Are almost as enchanting as those upon the hill
I water them and talk to them until
They flourish and my heart they fill.

Rhyme for a Rose

Roses are not so easy to grow
And the hot-house varieties have no scent.
But that's the best part God had to bestow,
Tho' the gorgeous colors make them so pleasant.

A rose by any other name would smell as sweet—
Shakespeare knew his subject.
A rose is one of nature's finest works of art
And my garden's so bedecked.

Forsythia

Gorgeous yellow forsythia
You are the harbinger of Spring!
Long life and copious blooms I wish for ya
You make my wintry heart sing.

I spy you from my window
And delight in every change you make.
I chart your course in winter, covered with snow,
Throughout the summer, when you bake.

Most of all, of course, the magnificent Spring
When you come into your glory for all to see.
You're quite exquisite, little forsythia tree,
And I like to pretend you bloom just for.

What a Beautiful World

What a beautiful world You've made, Lord:
That's not an original observation;
I know untold billions of people have said it
With varying degrees of elation.

The tranquility of the water,
The splendor of the sky,
The green stretches on for miles,
I want to take it with me when I die.

Oh, I know Your Heaven is more marvelous
But how can it ever surpass this lovely world?
It defies the imagination to even contemplate
A more magnificent landscape unfurled.

Lord, give me the eyes to comprehend
The grandeur and glory of Heaven;
Give me the heart to appreciate
That beauty seventy times seven.

What a beautiful world You've made, Lord,
And given to me for my appreciation;
I'll enjoy it till Heaven comes along,
Then I'll welcome *that* with utmost anticipation.

ABOUT ME

Private *Personal*

Just between you and me....

Aerie

Our own little eagle's nest, an aerie, if you will,
Situated high up on a mountain;
That's how I feel about our little home,
All that's missing is a pool and fountain!

It's a place of refuge from cares and woes,
A place where Jesus meets you daily;
When you stop and call on Him
He will come along-side you, gaily.

A deck overlooking town and country,
Even a view of the hospital—how's that for security?
The deer and magnificent foliage,
All portrayed with breathtaking purity.

I feel a comfort I've not always experienced
A peace passing all understanding.
The love of the Lord and of family
Is always and forever outstanding!

My Deck

The Old Front Porch has morphed into a wooden deck
Perched half-way up the side of a mountain.
The view from here is absolutely stupendous
'Tho there's no view of sparkling lake or fountain.

Lounging on the deck is being close to heaven;
One feels relaxed and so at peace.
A place for reading and day-dreaming,
The site where all one's cares must cease.

And yet a perfect spot for reminiscing,
For prayer, both asking and receiving.
For contemplation, praise, and pleading,
Entreating—a location for believing.

My deck: a church, a home, a sanctuary,
A living room, sunroom, at times a dining room.
A hundred different things to different people
It sweeps away one's problems like a broom.

Most of all, the place one welcomes Jesus,
To come and sit and chat and stay a while.
And always, rain or shine or windstorm,
My deck's the place that ever makes me smile.

Jesus sometimes comes and sits there, also.
He loves to meet His children where they are.
Conversing with us, in a friendly manner,
We're ever the best of friends, by far.

Contrasts

I've been close to the Arctic Circle,
And visited Key West.
Contrasts are not new to me
I'd never say which one is best.

I've huddled in below zero weather
Feeling frozen to the bone.
I've basked on a tropical beach
Until my skin fairly shone.

I've had marriage and children,
I've experienced wedded bliss;
I've been single many years now—
Sometimes married life I miss.

I've been in groups too large to bear,
I've been alone and very lonesome;
I've felt lonely in a crowd,
And there were times alone is awesome!

Life is always full of contrasts.
Who wants a life all monochrome?
Rejoice in good, bad, highs and lows.
Exult in raucous music or a quiet poem.

Cuddly Pals

I've written of my bed buddies,
And told you of my "Red",
And all the cuddly critters
I've brought into my bed.

After a long hiatus, as it were,
My "Red" returned a while ago,
To join my soft and sweet green turtle,
Without whom I couldn't sleep, you know.

I'm a very tactile person
And they're so soft and silky to the touch.
Needless to say, though it may sound silly,
I love both of them very much.

Complaining

Now I know why old folks like to complain!
Nobody listens, it's true (but it's sometimes fun to do).
And aches and pains are all we have, for the most part,
So, what else is there to discuss that is new?

I tell my friends and family to tell me when I complain,
But it feels like I'm just conversing, don't you know?
Perhaps I am unaware when my attitude sounds negative
I truly don't mean to, it could be when I'm feeling low.

Occasionally, one simply needs to vent.
At times one needs to get it off one's chest, so to speak.
Or it could be that another's waiting for you to identify
With him, and empathize, and not feel so unique.

So, that's my excuse for from time to time complaining.
I try not to do that, but it too often happens, I'm told.
Too many times I am caught in that predicament,
What's your excuse? I'm old!

Exercise in Futility

Night after night, I play Solitaire on my computer,
Striving to beat the odds and increase my wins.
As if anyone in the world will ever see my statistics,
As if anyone knows when it ends or begins.
It's an exercise in futility.

Day after day I get up in the morning,
I dress myself and perform my daily ablutions,
As if there was someone watching to be sure that I did it;
As if to all the world's problems my habits were the solutions.
Another exercise in futility.

They say the definition of madness is doing the same
Thing over and over, expecting a different ending;
Tilting at windmills, trying to make a big difference,
I'm still watching the world in all its upending.
Watching it all in its futility.

But never expecting to be or do anything significant,
Never trying anything because no one cares,
Is to never find happiness within my own existence;
It's never being that courageous one who dares
To experience that exercise in futility.

Do You Feel Me?

Do you feel me?
In modern parlance many say this;
It is so expressive. What's it all about?
Not sympathy, but empathy;
Something subtle—no need to shout.

Can you feel me?
Can you feel another's pain,
Their hurt, their love, their joy?
Can you feel me when I try so hard
To convey what's inside me?
Can you know what I'm about?
Do you know my subtleties?
Am I an open book?

Can you feel me?
Can you understand what I am all about?
Can you see inside me,
At the courage and the doubt?
I want to feel the happiness inside you,
Welling up and sometimes spilling over.
Or that ache that you keep deeply hidden.
I can tell you are not romping in the clover.

Can we really feel each other,
Our hopes, our plans, our dreams?
Can we go dancing in the cornfields?
Can we go skipping in the streams?
Can we really know each other?
Can we understand at all
What it's like to be you,
What it means to be me?
Can you feel me?
Do you really, really feel me?

Elemental

I'm getting rather maudlin—
Just pensive isn't the case.
I seem to be reflecting more these days
Now that I'm nearing the end of my race.

I'm thinking back on regrets of the past,
I'm remembering a happier time;
I'm wishing for things that I never had—
That's not my usual paradigm!

Perhaps I am just being honest with myself,
Admitting the dreams I once had.
But dreams are for youngsters—
Maybe this is all just a fad.

I am not usually so mawkish and sappy,
Nor prone to be overly sentimental.
But we all have our moments, our hours, our days—
That's the human condition—elemental.

Trust

I pray for trust in You, my God—
This is not so much a poem as a prayer;
I am discouraged—I don't want to be, You know that.
My faith has not always been there.

My discouragement comes because I do not trust enough;
Why? You have always, always come through for me and mine.
I have no logical reason not to trust You,
You constantly have filled me with Your new wine.

I beg You, Lord, to help my unbelief!
Increase my flagging faith, abolish all my doubt.
Though situations may look dark and hopeless,
I have no rational cause to rant and shout.

I have full confidence in what You have in store,
I really do put all my faith in You—I must!
You have the only answers for me, my city and my world,
But please, Almighty God, help me to trust!

Frustration

Frustration makes me want to cry,
But why, oh, why do I want to cry?
Is it lack of control when problems pass by
Or something quite different— I sigh!

Is it wanting to handle *everything*
To prove I can manage what life can bring?
It's certainly not wanting to act like a King,
Or always craving a little zing!

Why do I cry when I'm frustrated?
Why pound my fist and get agitated?
I thought I was long since emancipated,
That worries and problems had all abated.

But here I am again in another situation
Wherein I'm not experiencing much elation!
In fact, there's just no correlation
Between happiness and intense frustration.

I wish I was smart and knew it all,
Or had a genius on whom to call,
So, I could climb above it all
And not forever and always fall!

Why does frustration make me cry?
I can't control it, I just want to sigh,
And make all my frustrations go bye-bye;
But I can't, and I don't, so I guess I'll just cry!

Give it Up

I'll never see the Bridge in San Francisco
Or get a glimpse of Alcatraz across the Bay;
Visiting the pyramids is just not in my future,
I'd love to see the Holy Land, but, no way!

I used to dream of going to Australia,
Or sailing to a hot and tropic land;
I've always had a soft spot for the ocean
And sinking my little tootsies in the sand.

I know I'll never ever climb a mountain,
Or bungee jump from a gigantic bridge;
I'm not about to swim the English Channel,
Or ski down some tall and winding ridge.

I can't compete with Thomas Kincade's paintings
Or ever write another "Wuthering Heights";
I can't imagine singing at the opera
Or experiencing a diva's joys and plights.

Long-gone are some of the simpler enjoyments,
Like experiencing romantic love and all its pleasures;
But in my heart, are such marvelous memories,
And in my mind, I store up all those treasures.

No life is lived without some fleeting happiness.
We all should cherish even the most mundane,
Not dwell on all the things we didn't achieve,
But in every instance, count it all as gain.

Whether at the start or end of this life-journey,
Give up all sorrow and regrets and that which grieves us,
Knowing somehow everything will be all right
If we simply give our all to Jesus.

First and Last

It's been a while, I think you'd agree,
But I'm not over you yet.
I don't know where or how you are,
But you never think of me, I'll bet.

It was probably all a fantasy,
I was "in love with love", or so they say,
But you have to admit you teased me,
I really thought we would have our day.

You had good and kind and loving
Down to a science, as it were,
Sweet and solicitous and godly,
Always a gentleman, sir.

But, enough! This is not productive.
I'm just indulging in remembering the past.
In case you ever wonder,
You were my first love and my last.

I Am an Anchor

I am an anchor in a turbulent sea,
I am a harbor sheltered from the elements;
Friend and acquaintance can rely on me.
I am a rock on which one may lean,
A resting place that's warm and secure
Against all dangers seen and unseen.

I am *no* anchor, but a vacillating weed
Bobbing and weaving on that frothing sea,
Searching for an anchor to cling to in *my* need.
Where are all those who leaned on me
When I want to lean, in *my* weariness,
And feel safe and secure from that tumultuous sea?

But, I am an anchor! I have to be—
For that is my excuse for existence.

Basking

Don't call me a "sun worshipper"—
I dislike that—a lot!
Worship the sun I do not.
Basking in the sunshine just "hits the spot".
Enjoying its light and heat—that you've got!
Even when others say it's way too hot
The peace and solace of the sun I've sought;
I need the tranquility that has brought.
Basking is a delightful word I like a lot.

Imagined Kisses

I cannot remember when I was last kissed,
In a romantic, meaningful way,
By someone who really loved me,
Or, at least explore the possibility.
Perhaps I never, truly was loved that way
By one who just didn't want to "make hay".

I am up in years now
But still can't help but wonder
If kissing is all it's "cracked up to be";
It makes me stop and ponder.
Maybe these feelings are just for the young—
Can't remember that far back yonder.

And so, I enjoy romantic comedies
And devour good, clean love-books
About cowboys, preachers, bankers and such,
Or sailors, singers or cooks.
I only sigh and imagine
All those soul-searching looks.

Such is the foolishness of women—
Or maybe men sometimes do it, too—
Fantasize about those kisses and hugs,
Or read romantic novels, in lieu.
But it's still fun to imagine
Someone softly saying, "I love you".

I Did

Twenty years from the day I was born
I looked and thought, "I could have".

At thirty years I awoke one morn
And said to myself, "I would have".

Forty years it took me to form
All the reasons I should have.

Lord, please let me awake
The last day of my life
    And look back and say.......... "I DID"!

Guardian Angel

I must have a guardian angel
That Jesus loves me so much.
He protects me in all my ways,
In chaos and turmoil and such.
He makes sure my Angel
Spreads wings over me,
Even in trouble, I feel His touch.
Someone once told me there was no God
And that I was using "religion" as a crutch.
Crutch, smutch, whatever you think,
I KNOW Jesus loves me very much.

Imaginary Lover

In my lonely room, night after night,
My heart dreams of another,
My body anticipates the touch
Of an imaginary lover.

Part made up of whole-cloth,
Part remembrance from the past.
I cannot separate the two,
And yet my die is cast.

I sometimes can embrace the dream.
And conjure many others;
Most often, I awaken, serene
Envisioning my imaginary lover.

Inanity

Here I go again,
Doing what I do, and then
Doing it all over again.
The definition of insanity?
Or, perhaps, just inanity?
But doing what I know how to do
Is comfortable, you know it's true.
What else to do, I haven't a clue.

I Don't Feel Old

I can't say I really know
What feeling old is like,
And dwelling on the negative
Is something I dislike.

Oh yes, sometime I feel
A little under the weather,
And often more than one of my conditions
Collide and come together.

But old? Not really.
I usually feel very youthful;
I seldom feel my age at all—
And, mostly, I am truthful.

They say age is just a state of mind.
How old you think you are—you are!
I never want to be *really* young again—
I know to some, that is definitely bizarre!

Everything that's gone on in the past—
I'm grateful for the journey I've had.
It all has made me who I am—
I'm thankful for the good and the bad.

I Don't Feel Old (cont'd)

Now I've achieved an age once unheard of.
I could never have imagined the number I would reach.
Each year of my life was a learning experience,
So now, I believe, I am ready to teach.

I still say that I don't feel old,
And that I adamantly maintain!
Tho' I will not be, or look it,
I'll feel young all the days that remain.

I've Never Seen

I've never seen the heather on a Scottish moor,
Nor all the vivid greens that Ireland's famous for;
I've never watched the powerful surfers on Hawaii's shore,
Nor enjoyed the graceful dancers on a ballroom floor.
I'm fortunate not to have witnessed a devastating war,
Or undergone the hardships of those days of yore.
I've never gone to exotic places to explore,
Nor been presented to dignitaries, their favors to implore.
But one day I will see the King that I adore!!

Life Goes On

I was at a Little League field
While my Mom lay in the hospital, dying.
I had to bring my boys back home
At the end of the game, but I was crying.
        Life goes on.

I had three children to care for
Without the Mom we all adored;
Even tho' my heart was breaking,
Giving in to self-pity I could not afford.
        Life goes on.

When the call came that I had lost my money,
The voice on the other end of the line
Was sad to have to tell me the news.
His was no sadder than mine.
        But life goes on.

The wedding was scheduled for Saturday.
It would have been an amazing day!
But she left me at the altar,
And no word did she say.
        Life goes on.

Getting into my car, all packed, ready to go.
We were to take that long-awaited trip to the shore,
When I was informed a close friend had died.
I had to go with my family—that's what Dads are for
        Life goes on.

I've survived fire, flood, and hurricanes, too,
Birth and death and much trauma,
The ups, downs, ins and outs of life:
I've encountered a plethora of drama
        Life goes on.

Make It Count

I gave myself the morning
To do whatever came to mind.
To sleep, to eat, to pray, to read,
Whatever pursuits I'd like to find.

I cherish so, the morning,
My time for rejuvenation.
I organize my mind, my day,
What glorious expectation!

Today I can do anything
My head and heart conjectures.
Write a startling treatise or
Fill the world with pretty pictures.

I can utilize the morning
Or sleep, and do without.
That's not what I want to do—
I'd rather make it count.

Little Dark Hole

I can feel myself burrowing down into my little dark hole.
I want to pull all the dirt down on me.
I want everything outside of me to be silent;
I want the whole world to stop instantly!

I curl up in my comfortable bed,
My warm, soft blankets surround,
The fetal position's my favorite pose,
With my pillows and stuffed animals around.

Or, I sit in my cozy recliner,
Tucked into the corner of my room,
Gazing pensively out of my window,
Recumbent is the position I prefer to assume.

This little dark hole is so friendly
I really don't want to come out.
Reading or writing or sleeping—
Is this all that life is about?

Is this a form of depression?
My little dark hole's that, I reckon;
I'm awaiting something or someone
To speak to me, or just beckon.

I climb down into my little dark hole—
I am consciously seeking oblivion.
I surrender myself to the arms of Morpheus—
Is this what it's like in heaven?

My Children

I love my daughters very much
Both are quite unique
They threw away the mold, I know
So, don't anyone bother to seek.

They both have attributes far
Above their own understanding.
And both have lives, that up to now
Have been extremely demanding.

About my sons, I have a hard time
Even saying enough.
Let's just affirm, for starters.
None is a powder puff.

Through many ups and downs,
They were found upright.
And most of it was accomplished
Completely out of my sight.

They all are good men and true
To God and country and self.
All are ambitious, that I know,
And none will ever sit on the shelf.

My Greatest Success

I studied to be an English teacher.
Went to the Air Force, instead.
Trained to be a Drill Instructor,
Loud enough, not firm enough.

I aspired to be a writer,
But only wrote for myself.
I planned to be a good wife,
But fell way short of the mark.

I tried to be a good Mom,
But does any Mom feel good enough?
I thought I was a good friend—
Some say Yes, some No.

I once thought I was a singer,
But chance and age finished that.
I tried six different musical instruments,
Absolutely to no avail!

I studied Sign Language many years,
But fate brought me no one to sign to.
I wasn't even a very good lover,
Or so my mistakes seem to conclude.

But this isn't a litany of failure,
But of my greatest success, by far—
I believe I finally did things right—
I fell in love with Jesus!

Me, Myself and I

It's very intriguing, being Me
And always interesting, you see,
For if I really couldn't be Me
Who in the world would I get to be?

I am completely happy, being Myself,
And not an alien or little elf;
I don't care to be an object on a shelf.
I'm reconciled to this thing called "self".

I'm eminently satisfied with being I.
Not everyone is, you cannot deny.
I could probably be better—that I buy,
But I accept Me, Myself, and I.

Letting Go

Today I "left my kids at camp",
Or so it feels to me.
I consigned a batch of paintings
To a place that wants to see
If we can help each other
And profit mutually.
So, for a while my walls are naked
And my "loving arms" feel empty.
But soon my fingers will paint once more
And my imagination, once again, fly free!

Proud to Blush

I heard a word on the subway
My face turned a lovely shade of red,
Not the word so much—I'd heard it before—
But not quite so blatantly said.
   I am happy I can still blush.

Sunbathing by the poolside,
Some teens blasted their radios.
I'd never heard lyrics like that before,
It certainly jarred me from my repose.
   I am glad I can still be appalled.

I watched a movie with my granddaughter;
At first it was funny, then…not.
I was taken aback at the content—
Against my innate prudishness I fought.
   But I'm proud I can still blush.

I accessed a social media page
A grandson sent me a joke.
Horrified, shocked—I can't express it!
I wish that time I could revoke.
   It still colors our relationship.

I was deep into a great love story,
Much absorbed with its great plot,
Until it went beyond the bounds of good taste.
Could I finish the book—I think not!
   Can one blush with one's whole body?

Right for Me

A little like his father,
A little like his Mom,
A little like the boy next door,
Accepting that with aplomb.

Something of a "bad boy"
A rake, a gigolo, roué
Very much the consummate mensch, *
Player by night, gentleman by day.

Whatever you say about him
He is someone you can love.
He will always be there for you;
You fit like a hand in a glove.

The epitome of a young girl's dream
He's all that you want him to be.
Whatever his faults or foibles
He's always just right for me.

*Yiddish for gentleman

See Me

See me, Dad, please see me!
Recognize who I am and can be.
Not merely an extension of yourself—
Tell me you have confidence in me,
That I will do what I'm meant to do
And be what I'm meant to be.
Realize my full potential,
Not just as your offspring, but as Me.

See me, Love, please see me!
Open your heart and your eyes;
See my love and yearning,
I am not in disguise.
Realize who I am inside,
Who I want to be to you.
Oh, the angst of disappearing from view,
Of having you look and talk to me
And see your eyes are shuttered and blank—
You really do not see me!

See me, World, please see me!
Not simply what I can offer you.
Look into my heart and mind,
Acknowledge all that I can and will do.
I am a complicated composite
Of all God has destined and ordained;
Not only what is seen on the surface,
But of all that is in me contained.

See Me (cont'd)

I am not merely flesh and muscle.
I'm more than beauty or stature;
I am intelligent, confident, benevolent,
More than any exterior feature.
See me, the Me inside of me,
To the very core of my being.
Take time to really see me—
Not just look, but really see me!

I know, Lord, that You see me,
Down to my soul and marrow and bone.
Keep me always transparent to You
And I'll never feel alone.
You alone can grasp what I am
And fathom all I am meant to be.
I believe only You can truly know
And really, really, see me!

Role Model

You are the best role model I could ever have,
Even though you don't want to be.
I like to emulate you in actions and ways
While still being uniquely me.

Oh, you may slip every once in a while,
But that's also understood;
It just shows that you're human,
And I think it's all good.

I admire your patience, and handling stress,
Your perseverance in times of trials.
You have learned a lot about life and love
You have really clocked up the miles.

Your love and compassion
Stands you in good stead;
You filter everything on the basis of that
And somehow, you come out ahead.

You are my role model,
Though I'm older than you;
I have more mileage than anyone dreamed,
But I will always look up to you.

Painting, Pottery, Plants and Poetry

Unlikely bedfellows, some might say.
Nevertheless, untold times they have made my day.
Most often when the Muse I choose to obey.

I know that it's God Who inspires my rhymes;
He gives me the subjects for my paintings, at times;
And how awe-inspiring to watch as my philodendron climbs.

The pottery—not so much creating as painting them,
Embellishing each as I would God's hem,
And praying over all as I create an imperfect gem.

I so enjoy painting ceramics, crosses and such,
And painting my canvases by the bunch,
But penning my poems I love so much!

I like to watch my plants flourish and bloom,
Brightening up my life as well as my room,
Eradicating any and all signs of gloom.

My paintings reflect words from the Lord,
My poetry's inspired by life and His Word—
Paintings, Pottery, Plants, Poetry—all in one accord.

Shell

It's hard to remember a time there were no tears, no sorrow
　　On the surface or hidden just beneath.
It's hard to remember the happy times we had, the sweet love,
　　The passion, the poignant memories.
It's easier to remember the bitterness, the hate,
　　The disappointments, betrayals, agonies, defeat.

After a time, as with most of us, a shell began to form
　　Around my heart and my emotions.
I am afraid of love and happiness for fear
　　Of rediscovering the tears.
Until, at night, sometimes I yearn for the refreshing release
　　Of being able to shed those tears that lie in wait
Just below the hardened surface of my emotional shell.

New Way to Be

I am getting adjusted to a brand-new me
After years of being a dedicated "groupie"
And living and loving down by the sea.
I am learning a new way to be.

I am experiencing a new way to exist.
I no longer need or want to be kissed.
I am a bit more existential,
Though some latent yearnings tend to persist.

I'm learning it's all right to be true to me,
I no longer just sit and observe from the shelf.
I am, simply, me, and it's all right to be,
I'm now so much more aware of self.

Tears

What are these droplets in my eyes?
I feel my eyes are leaking.
Whether from a blessing or a sadness,
Havoc it is wreaking.

A song, a scent, a memory—
Solace I am seeking.
I really do not want to cry,
It's always so unnerving.

I try returning to my happy place
But my thoughts continue swerving.
Over my leaking eyes I have no control,
Of a respite I am most deserving.

Smiling Picture

I'm looking at your photograph,
You're perched upon a wall.
Smiling is your countenance,
You are like a Barbie Doll.
You seem to be so carefree,
So happy, all-in-all.
I hope you keep that gay façade
That seeming joy, withal;
Most of all, I pray for you,
That you never, ever fall.

Should

I don't believe in "should".
Oh, you should go to that
Because it's expected of you;
Or, you should be there
Because it's their due.
So, when did life become
All about another's view?

I abhor the word "should".
But more, the reason behind.
I do believe in "should"
When I know God wouldn't mind;
When I am sure those around me
Would be responding in kind.

When other's opinions and mores
Interfere with what I do,
When I allow society
To dictate my actions and view—
And without conscious thought on my part
My own opinions I eschew.

You should do this, you should do that.
I want to be a thinking man.
I won't be a pre-programmed robot,
I want to live within God's plan.
He expects me to think for myself, so,
These stipulations I will ban.

Should (cont'd)

I never want to be controlled
By anyone but the Lord.
He gave me a mind to think with;
He also gave me His Word.
Society should not control me—
I have His Shield and His Sword.

There's that "should" word again.
I'll substitute with will.
I will do what I know to be right,
My spirit no one can kill;
I will be and do what I'm meant to:
Only God can that instill.

I am through allowing others to dictate.
I'll not be a slave to society.
I will do what I am meant to do,
And what is right for me.
No longer will I in any way
Let life "should" all over me!

Tapestry

You are but a tiny thread on the underside of this weaving—
This beautiful, gigantic, complicated tapestry we call Life.
From here it just looks like a bunch of tangled knots,
Full of trouble, controversy, pain and debilitating strife.

But we know the Master Weaver and we know that one day soon
He will complete this tapestry, smoothing out the rough places;
Your insignificant portion of this much larger piece
Will finally makes sense, with all its curves and spots and spaces.

So, do not simply focus on this knotted, tangled, woven work,
But concentrate on the correct stitches and use the proper thread.
The workmanship will be perfect, your sewing even above par,
If you will only use the materials He's provided.

Self-Description

I love the crazy words I use to describe myself:
Galloping Grumpies, Quarky, Wonky come to mind.
Different and discombobulated still apply,
There's many other words I often find.

But, I'm just me, like any other person.
I'm not really unusual or unique.
I like to think I am, and I may be at times,
But it's simply for acceptance that I seek.

I'm a million things, as most human beings are,
I'll try not to be too squirrelly, stoic or strange.
I'll just be myself in the future,
But in the blink of an eye that could change!

Fleeting Years

The years between youth and old age
Are flitting and fleeting, at best.
It seems the day after you're married
The "birds" are leaving the nest.

Some events, of course, are memorable
But more often than not are forgettable.
Some, I must say, are regrettable,
But try as we may, are ephemeral.

Only a photographic memory
Can recapture the past at will.
But, then, do we really want to recall
Those youthful thoughts when we're "over the hill"?

Unrequited Love

Unrequited love is frequent fodder
For lonely-hearted readers and writers of verse.
Without that subject there would be fewer novels,
Less plays and poetry—and what is worse—

"Romeo and Juliet" would never have been penned;
But that's not something to which I am averse.
Love that has not goal nor outlet
Is really something of a curse.

If not for loneliness and cheating hearts and such
Where on earth, I ask you, would songwriters be?
Their foremost stock in trade's that very subject:
Sorrow, angst, pain and infidelity.

We often dwell on unrequited love,
But few who have experienced it are happy.
It makes us yearn for what might have been—
To have loved and lost is not a pleasant place to be.

Yes, we delight in reading of unrequited love;
Mostly, because it comes out right in the end.
But love that keeps on longing for another,
That's not so "delightful", and very hard to mend.

Up in Years

It's really not so bad being up in years—
As I read about others' trials and tribulations
I suddenly think, I'll never again have to worry
About those horrendous situations.

I hear talk about politics on TV and the papers—
I needn't be so concerned with all of that.
Not that I don't care, just not so much;
It's all just bothersome, like a gnat.

See a handsome hunk on the street or TV
And begin to dream a little still.
Then I remind myself, it's really good
Not to have to "go there" again. I will

Not worry about how I look to him,
Or what I'd say if he *did* "like me"
It's kind of cool to be old!
And that's how it is with me.

I can always play the "old" card
And get away with it, too.
Until I run into someone much older
Who's making a difference, it's true.

So, I shouldn't just rest on being old!
Tho' it's kinda cool to be up in years.
I still need to get up and get out there,
And not succumb to my trivial fears.

Wannabee

Why am I a Wannabee?
Never, truly, a writer-bee,
Or potter or a painter-bee?
I'm only ever close, you see
To achieving what I wannabee.

I was once a mama bee
Trying to make my children be
All they were ever meant to be,
To allow them their own identity
And, hopefully, then, reflect on me.

I wrote a lot of poetry
I made a lot of pottery,
I painted canvases that personify me
And journaled much, for posterity:
But I know I was just a wannabee.

One thing never fell into that category:
I was a Christian, categorically!
I never compromised my integrity,
Or denied my Lord, e'en strategically.
I loved Him always, positively,
And will be His for eternity!

So, I am not sad, definitely!
I have finally found what I wannabee:
To live for the Lord, and apparently,
That is what He meant me to be,
And the other things that I tried to be
I know were as He intended, ultimately.

Sneaky

I put my veggies in my pocket,
Went to the outhouse to dispose,
That probably began my life
Of sneakiness, I suppose.

Hid a piece of pie behind my back
So my husband wouldn't know it was my second;
Guess I was still being a sneak,
One never really grows up, I reckon.

Looked for my Christmas presents early
Is that, too, a symptom of being a sneak?
Curiosity is what I call it,
I merely wanted a teensy little peek.

I believe sneakiness is really the norm.
It's part and parcel of life.
Does everyone experience this
Or is it just peculiar to a wife?

It's not simply being a "private person"
It's really being a sneak.
But in my own defense, as it were,
Perhaps it's just acceptance that I seek.

Insomniac

The world is a very different place at night,
Even in the confines of my darkened room.
It can be a bright, light Palace stage
Or feel like a warm, embracing womb.
I can endeavor to encompass it all,
Or lie stiff and silent as in a tomb.

I've tried to sing myself to sleep,
I've arisen and gotten up to work,
That seems to be best, because work's never done,
And no one could say I would shirk.
If I lie still much longer, I know,
I will be bound to go berserk!

I've exercised, and showered, also,
Changed my bedding and re-arranged my room.
I've done all I can think to do,
And still the shadows loom.
I fervently wish for daylight,
To see the lovely flowers bloom.

I've watched a TV show or two
And sometimes read a whole book.
I'm wrapped up in the tale, you know,
All thoughts of sleep I've forsook.
Then when I finally close my eyes,
Wraiths are everywhere I look.

Insomniac (cont'd)

I lie down once again, on my bed,
My eyes are heavy, my body tired,
I curl up in my welcoming, cozy covers—
God knows I certainly tried!
My traitorous eyes pop open wide,
Once again in fantasies I'm mired.

I ruminate on what I want from the future,
And meditate about what I once was, looking back.
I imagine myself with a beautiful babe,
In a long, fancy yacht or a black Cadillac:
It's then I know these are all delusions,
The creative ramblings of a raving insomniac!

Contemplation

When I'm not feeling up-to-par I contemplate my demise.
I think of who to contact and who will pay my bills,
And what if my next of kin doesn't know what to do:
All that may sound helpful, but rarely ever wise.

I've been told by many that I am a control freak.
I've contemplated that, and think it must be very true.
But if it's all the same to you, I prefer another name;
I'd rather be known as simply being quite unique.

Colors

I love to mix the colors
To see what tint emerges
I enjoy the colors on my brush
In answer to my urges.

Purple is a royal color,
A haughty color, too.
Many, many shades there are,
From richest red to blue.

There's much in the color purple,
That I find hard to explain;
But there's one I am not fond of:
The color puce, I do disdain.

My favorite's probably fuchsia,
And then, perhaps, lime green.
I love fluorescent colors,
But they're not usually in a scene.

I enjoy all the pastel colors,
Light blue, and pink and yellow,
But warm browns and burnt oranges
Are pleasing, and so mellow.

I love the whole palette of the greens,
They fit into any kind of venue;
I also like the jewel tones:
Red and green and blue.

Let's face it—I like colors,
Not so much the black and white,
Although they wouldn't be there
If not for the dark and light.

Decision

When I made the decision to serve my country
It was more about me than about Him.
When I made the decision to marry,
It may have been more on a whim:
I wanted many children, and felt this
Was the way to do it without living in sin.
Yes, I'm a prude, you may have discerned by now,
By some of the poems that have appeared herein.

My life decisions have not all been
Arrived at so whimsically.
For the most part, I've prayed about them
And He was included, intrinsically.
It's really an educated decision
I arrive at most naturally.
And He is most certainly consulted
I am part of Him and He of me.

I write this to inform you
Of the most important decision that can ever be:
Certainly, I've made my share of wrong ones,
But more right than not, gratefully.
The greatest decision I've ever made,
The most important one, that always pleases,
And no one ever goes wrong in making,
Is the decision I made—to follow Jesus!

My Brain is Full

Cease the madness! Stop the persistent bombardment,
The continual barrage of thoughts, pictures and dreams;
My brain is full! I cry, cease and desist!
After all these years I retain everything, it seems!
Ideas, quotations, phrases, facts and fictions,
Photos and fragments and glimpses and gleams.

When my eyes are open or whether they're closed
Through my mind they are whirling at a fantastic speed.
Lists I am making, trips I am taking, my body is aching,
But still it continues, that gigantic kaleidoscope I feed
With all my musings, meanderings, memories—
And they're not all always real, I have to concede.

My imagination is active, and that's as it should be,
My intellect's really a force of its own:
Didactic, moralistic, romantic, futuristic;
I see the past and the present and e'en the unknown.
It's like some gigantic motion picture screen,
But when I awaken, I find it's all flown.

I just can't stop the thinking, the plans, the designs,
Embracing my remembrances, forecasting the future,
I am ever projecting, organizing, arranging
Schedules and schemes, I constantly nurture.
For my life, my future, my present and past
I am really the penultimate researcher.

My Brain Is Full (cont'd)

Imagine a college student—what he has already learned
And all he has lived, and watched and experienced!
Then double that panorama alive in his brain,
And factor in all he has thought and sensed,
Witnessed and daydreamed and put down on paper,
For which he feels he has amply been recompensed.

Cease this outpouring, my brain is so full!
I must stop this onslaught, it's disturbing my sleep!
Yes, I want to remember, I enjoy some of the dreams,
But too much of a good thing on my head it does heap!
If I am being assaulted—that's what I call it—
Quickly and soon out of bed I must leap!

I am glad for the memories and all the slideshows
That play out through my mind at a frantic pace,
But the timing's not right, it's just not the time,
And it's definitely not the appropriate place!
When I lie down at night, courting sweet repose,
Could we just put a hold on that feverish race?

PENSIVE

Thought Provoking

Reflective

Philosophical

Acceptance

Have you attained the life you desired
Or accepted the life you were given?
Have you settled for mediocrity
Or achieved that for which you have striven?

Have the goals you set for yourself been
           realized?
Have your glorious plans come to fruition?
Have you settled and drifted and coasted,
Has your life really come to completion?

It's never too late to reach for the stars
You're never too old to change course.
   Your dreams can come true
   It's all up to you
Or accept it for better or worse.

Passing Minutes

The minutes keep on passing,
No stopping them, no slowing down
Sometimes it seems they're dragging,
At times you look up and they've flown.

Ambivalent

I'm very ambivalent today.
Don't know where I am or who.
Can't tell why I'm really here
Or what I'm supposed to do.
Should I write or should I paint?
Perhaps there's another project
I am supposed to pursue.

At times I do two things at once,
Am I "biting off more than I can chew"?
I don't think that's multi-tasking,
My mind just grabs on to something new.
Should I cancel one, that's all I'm asking.
Is ambivalence a blessing or a curse?
Can it turn my life askew?

Could I accomplish much today,
Or maybe a feat of derring-do?
Wish I could get on-target for once,
If only the target was something I knew.
Perhaps I am over-thinking here.
Should I simply relax and roll with it?
Am I making, as they say, too much ado?

Care-Full Woman

Sadness settled gently on her shoulders,
Sorrow seemed to be so fitting there.
Worry was imprinted on her forehead
As she quietly made room for one more care.

A line for every tear she'd ever shed.
Every tragedy in life was there reflected
In every silver hair upon her head—
But then she smiled!

Blessing of Forgetfulness

To be able to forget is often a blessing,
Else one might become a whiney one,
A mournful or contentious person,
Bitter, unforgiving, completely undone.
Forgetting can be a gift in itself.
It is peaceful to forget when day is done
And your brain insists on remembering
All the hurts you've received under the sun.
Then it is when you realize the blessing
Of selective forgetfulness—this game you've won!

Candles

Candle light,
    What a sight,
        Flames flickering
            In the night.
                It is all so lovely
                    And just seems so right.

The scent is so pleasant,
    It's not too much,
        Pine and lavender and vanilla and such,
            Ginger and sage and orange and spice;
                I love candles—they're oh, so nice!

Tapers, jars, pillars and floating ones,
    Tall ones, skinny ones, tiny tealights;
        Fat ones, square ones, all are delights.
            Some so unique you hesitate to burn,
                But you light each one—they take their turn.

Candles evoke a feeling
    That one can never define.
        They're spiritual, yet erotic, too;
            Romantic, oh, yes,
                But sometimes make you blue.
                    I do so love candles, don't you?

Corridors

I'm in a very different world,
Running down the corridors of my mind.
I dance, I skip, I leap, I whirl,
I open the doors that I'm hiding behind.

These corridors lead to fascinating places,
Some of which, I vow, I have declined.
But halls are ever for traveling down
Even when you are not so inclined.

Corridors are to bring you to a place,
You wish you were or would like to be.
Your mind is a terrible thing to waste,
But at times it goes off on a tangent, indubitably!

Sometimes those long, dark corridors
Are not such pleasant places to travel.
You can watch things you do not want to see
And watch your subconscious unravel.

But most of the time you experience joy
And pleasant places, if you start "free-wheeling".
Those eclectic corridors of your mind
Are all about hope and feeling.

Grief Is Selfish

There's nothing much more selfish than grief.
We really are mourning for ourselves.
Tho' tears and sobbing does grant some relief,
That sadness we are feeling's for ourselves.

If the person was not worthy—and who are we to say?
At least it is cessation from the pain.
We really wouldn't want to have it any other way:
Everyone deserves a peaceful, quiet death.

If he was really ready, a blessed child of God,
We know he will be welcomed into the Kingdom,
So, we should then be happy to see his just reward
And not be grieving quite so long and hard.

No, we are mourning mostly for the surcease
Of all the things that person meant to us,
And everything that will be missing in our lives—
So many things so bright and beauteous!

Having Fun

Having fun has changed the way it feels
That effervescent, giddy, bubbly feeling
Has been replaced, they say, with something
Sweeter, calmer, but still has your senses reeling.

Kiddie-fun we may still, at times enjoy
Like roller coasters or boating in the creek,
Swinging or playing ball with a child,
Hide-and-go-seek—now don't you peek!

Merely sitting down in the shade with a book,
Gives enormous enjoyment for one
Who simply appreciates the quieter things in life,
No longer wanting to sprint or romp or run.

A conversation with one whose company you value,
On subjects of interest to you both,
Is invigorating, energizing and, yes, fun—
When it's stimulating, not just air and froth.

Yes, indubitably, the definition of fun has matured
As we do, perhaps to our detriment.
But fun is still fun and fun's where you find it
And that, after all, is what makes us content.

Hurry!

You certainly can't hurry in a wheelchair,
You indubitably can't run with a cane,
You cannot rush about with a walker,
To endeavor to do so would be insane.
Perhaps in a power chair you can manage
To hurry just a little. You might gain
A few more steps than with a walker
But then you're back to square one again.
But thinking you can hurry when you can't
Is absolutely, positively inane.
It's important to remember at this stage of life
That slow and steady is the name of the game.

If Only

Two of the saddest words I know,
Along with rejection and lonely,
Are two little words I hear everyone say
Every day of their lives—if only!

Longevity

Longevity's such a fabulous word—
It rolls right off the tongue!
More marvelous, though, is the fact
That's the group I am among!

Instant Gratification

Instant coffee, instant oatmeal, instant gratification
of all kinds!
We can't wait a minute for anything!
We want it now and that goes for everything!

It takes too long to cook it, to mix it or wait for it.
We must instantly eat it
And instantly treat it.

We can't wait for a relationship to blossom.
We must follow our urges,
From sex to splurges.

Perhaps a little waiting would be a good thing.
Maybe then there'd be no sorrow tomorrow
Or trouble to borrow.

Instant gratification isn't all it's cracked up to be.
The food is *too* filling,
That "one" is *too* willing.

Grant me the patience to wait for a while.
To enjoy anticipation,
To allow for hesitation.
That's *real* gratification!

You Needn't Say You Love Me

When we're making love you needn't say you love me,
You needn't hold me tightly when we dance;
Don't laugh at all my jokes, they just aren't funny;
You're not obligated to speak words of romance,
You never have to say the word "forever",
I'll just assume it's there and take the chance.

The words won't matter to me if you're near me;
I won't ask anything of you on your part;
Inside I'll be imagining all those whispers,
Although I know it certainly isn't smart.
I'll feel all the tender words you aren't saying:
Fool that I am, I'll say them for you in my heart.

Language of Color

Purple's the color of royalty,
White the color of purity,
Blue is strength and honesty,
Yellow, of course, is sunniness,
Red the hue of cheerfulness;
Green is nature and coolness,
Aquamarine for harmony,
Magenta for vivacity,
Grey is for tranquility;
Orange for anything you want it to be
And black for nothingness.

Perception

Does anyone ever really see themselves as old?
Or pretty or homely or fat or bold?
Of course, the mirror shows all of the above
But perhaps we perceive through the eyes of love.

Once a friend, an overweight lady,
Confidentially to me revealed
I don't see myself as fat, tho' I know I am,
From my mind the truth was concealed.

I feel so much better now that I've lost weight
I've learned to love the body I once did hate.
But was I happier then not knowing I was obese?
Or now, knowing the overeating much cease?

Another acquaintance was truly emaciated,
Tho' every meal and snack were greatly anticipated.
He said, I really don't like myself quite this thin,
But the battle to gain weight I can't seem to win.

And age—now that's a real deception;
Everyone I know has a different perception.
One can be old and never even show it,
Or wrinkled and spotted and not even know it.

Some can seem to age at a very short clip,
While others reach 90 without even a blip.
Perhaps it really is, as they say, mostly mental.
A sweet attitude makes the aging more gentle.

Perception (cont'd)

Is one happier in ignorance—they say that's bliss,
But in not admitting faults one would be remiss.
Now we "see through a glass darkly",
Not perceiving ourselves quite so starkly.

Maybe one day our blinders will be lifted,
Out assets and flaws will then be sifted.
Till then, we can only go on as we are,
Perceiving our weaknesses from afar.

Perspective

If it doesn't kill you it may make you strong.
If it isn't right for you it could be wrong.
It might be something you should be doing all along.
If it doesn't shorten life, it still might not make it long.
If you don't look good in a bathing suit, don't wear a sarong.
If you can't carry a tune, you shouldn't sing a song.
The bell isn't ringing if you don't hear the gong.
Perhaps it's all about perspective, after all,
Or else life is all a bunch of folderol!

Pensive

Pensive is a thought-provoking word in itself.
First you wonder what it actually means,
And then if it truly applies to you.
It most often conjures up the vision
Of the famous statue of "The Thinker";
Perhaps he wasn't thinking, he was blue.
But was he actually sitting there reminiscing,
Or simply contemplating an exquisite view?

Procrastination

Procrastination may not be a sin, per se,
But it is a vice that besets most of humanity.
It is a rare individual that has never put things off
Until a time that fits more suitably!

Thou shalt not procrastinate is not in the Bible
But "Let your yea be yea"—comes to mind most frequently.
Saying you will do a task, then not performing it
At all, or in a timely manner, is just not "mannerly".

Practice saying what you'll do and won't do
Without waiting for a period more timely.
Is procrastination merely laziness?
Is it a fear you can't do a deed properly?

Is it pride or do you honestly forget
That promise that you've made so easily?
It's an automatic reaction, saying "Yes"
To one that you admire and want to please.

But do you know God calls that a lie
When you agree, then slough it off so breezily?
Try to think and pray before you answer
Or say "yes" to a request most casually.

Procrastination may not be a mortal sin,
But is certainly a fault, if done habitually.
Can you resolve to change that habit now,
Before it is that which you do perpetually?

Railing Against War

War is dirty, dark and deadly.
Whether on the streets or overseas,
Not glorious, not pretty,
It brings you to your knees.
Man's inhumanity to man is legendary
Sometimes it seems necessary, but is it?
Could there be another way?

Scrubbing floors with a toothbrush isn't fun,
For discipline, or to prove a point, perhaps.
G.I. Showers sound like overkill,
But they have their place.
War's not all about spit and polish,
Or simply seeking whom you may demolish;

It has its moments, very few,
When you are proud that you are you.
Soldier's Dilemma, in the Civil War,
Shell-shock in World War I and II,
Became PTSD in intervening wars—
Do you see the escalating horror in the terms?

A woman or man joins the military
To serve and fight for his country.
Patriotic it may seem at the time
Until he faces the enemy.
When you feel that bullet in your chest,
Even though you are wearing a vest,
It is painful, even deadly,
It's never very pretty.

Railing Against War (cont'd)

The blood and guts and gore you see
Were never, ever meant to be
A part of human history,
But there it is, for all to see.
It really is no mystery
The heinous crimes that man commits.

I didn't have to fight, but I could have;
I just don't know if I really would have.
When it's your life or another's
Perhaps we all are capable.

Living with that horror is quite another thing.
You join to fight the faceless enemy
But when you have to see his face
Things change!
Whether you're wounded or retire unscathed
You relive the memories all your life.
How you cope with all the images
Is a battle you may never win.

Living with someone who's gone through war
Is sometimes as traumatic as being there.
Knowing a soldier, a fireman, or policeman
Can be like experiencing it all yourself.
Some can empathize, and some just can't;
Some must distance themselves from it all.

Railing Against War (cont'd)

Wars and crimes and heinous acts
Have been prevalent down through the ages.
They are true. They happened frequently,
And not simply on book pages.
Who is right and who is wrong?
Which side the good side, which the bad?
Why can't men and women live peaceably
With their next-door neighbor?

If the "other guy" has differing values
Feels differently about life and liberty
Does it make it right that we should kill him?
Perhaps another way would be better,
But that's all we have, for now.

Standing up for ethical values,
Supporting a country that does,
Fighting for those who can't fight for themselves
That's who we are, after all.
But, no matter how you may rationalize,
We can beat this subject to death—and we do.
The beginning and end, since time immemorial
Leads to an inevitable conclusion:
War is Hell!

Relationship Dilemma

You see two people so "crazy in love"
They can't even see others around them.
You see the same two so hand-in-glove
That it appears it may be a problem

Then one day you're startled to behold
The same two, no longer together,
Both behaving so brash and bold,
Both seemingly straining at their tether.

Communication, they say, is the answer here,
But neither one seems to heed it.
They are locked in—in that space they adhere
To their own selfish wants—they need it.

One is not wrong, nor is the other.
There's times when they both seem right.
They just no longer seem to like one another
And the solution at the time is to fight.

They may not call it fighting, this thing that they do,
They're pursuing an amicable relationship.
If it was so amicable, would they split, the two,
Or try harder to concentrate on a friendship?

A cord once severed is very hard to mend.
A relationship is even more so.
Only God can repair it, in the end,
For we're flawed humans, here below.

Relationship Dilemma (cont'd)

Oh, pray for the couples who need a new start!
They can't seem to do it on their own.
Perhaps the answer is to develop a new heart,
One that isn't quite so "accident prone."

Now, I'm not espousing staying together
When the reasons the Bible clearly gives,
Nor if fear and abuse they must weather;
At times, apart is the way one must live.

One must pray always for a new insight
For those who are struggling to find the right way,
Because the human mind is always in flight,
Not knowing the answers for tomorrow or today.

Those around them watch with heavy heart,
Torn between the two so recently one,
Wondering if they their wisdom should impart
Or say, "there's nothing new under the sun".

Relationships are not merely a dilemma
For the couple involved, but for those
Who love and support them in their angst
And are anxiously waiting to see where it goes.

What changes between two so deeply in love?
Is it life, or circumstance, or humanity?
Is it a feeling from up above
Or simply human inanity?

Remembering

But, then, there is Remembering:
It's sometimes fun to do.
Remembering all the pleasant things
That have come to you.
And even some of the sad;
Happy memories sometimes bring a tear,
But not all tears are bad.

I love to remember people
Who have crossed my path.
There's really millions of them,
I cannot even do the math!
All the sweet things that have come my way
I will always be grateful for,
And I cherish to this day.

Chase That Dream

You can simply sleep with your dreams
Or wake up and chase them to their logical conclusion.
A dream is a God-given gift from above,
And should there ever be any confusion,
Your dreams are tailor-made for you,
And that's not simply a delusion.
They never come in one-size-fits-all,
And seldom in wonton profusion;
But I somehow doubt that if you don't pursue them
You'll never receive complete absolution.

Resentment

Resentment is a very harsh word
And it comes in many flavors.
You resent someone when they're mean to you
And resent them when they do you favors.

Resentment springs up at the oddest times,
When you least expect it to show.
For no conceivable reason it's there
And you let your mean-spiritedness flow.

Someone wants you to be independent
And leaves you to your own devices;
But you find yourself resenting them
When they're trying to be their nicest.

But if, on the other hand, they wait on you,
Taking care of you hand and foot,
You resent them for making you feel inept
And ignore all of their input.

Why is a human being so complex,
So contrary, or so it would seem?
To love and to hate in the very same breath,
So contradictory in the extreme!

I'd like not to resent people and things,
To always be very reasonable,
To never resent those who are doing their best.
Resentment is really unconscionable!

Ripples

Like ripples on the water,
Your lives have impacted many;
Your influence has touched
People that you know not of.
Numerous people everywhere
Have all been encouraged in some way,
Those motivated by your lives and care.
You'd be surprised if you could know
How many, how diverse they are;
In a round-about way your lives have been
The pebble God has tossed into the water
To begin the ripple, impacting so many lives
For Him.

Selective Sharing

We all select what we want to tell
And with whom we choose to share.
No one is completely transparent
We all embellish, we all compare.
We omit whole sections of our lives,
And no one is aware.
Most of us aren't really lying,
We're just relaying what we can bear.
Go on—you can tell all if you'd like to,
But if you do—beware!

So-o-o-o Long!

No one is very good at waiting
It just takes so-o-o-o long!
Not simply for the great occasions in life
But for the end of a story or of a song.

Some chalk it up to impatience
But I believe that's all wrong.
It's the little things that are the worst,
They just seem to take so-o-o-o long!

Waiting for the water to boil,
Or the microwave to ding,
Can seem like it takes hours,
When it's as quick as anything.

Waiting in the cold to catch a bus
May seem that it's so-o-o-o long,
But waiting for a painting to dry—
Now that really does take long!

Single Rose

A single rose in the vase;
It seems somehow stark and lonely.
Included, some greenery and a little card:
From the one who loves you, only

Shattered

Sometimes life doesn't break you
It shatters you like a pane of glass,
Broken into a zillion little pieces,
All a great, vast morass,
Leaving just a pile of shards
Congealing into a gelatinous mass.

It begins with just a miniscule crack
Zigzagging like lightning across the sky.
It start with the smallest pain
Or be caused by the tiniest lie
Whispered by one you thought loved you,
Shattered beyond wanting to die.

It's an earthquake of such magnitude
It cracks open your entire foundation—
A volcano erupting, spitting lava and fire,
Spewing down without cessation,
A tornado whirling and swirling away,
But when it ceases there is no elation.

Sometimes life must shatter a soul
To begin to fill in the pieces;
To mend all the broken remains
That have scattered to the far reaches;
Then sometime, somewhere, somehow,
Something or Someone finally frees us.

Slow Down

Are you too busy to be content,
Miss what's under your nose,
Because you are too busy staring at the stars,
Staring at the horizon, even in repose?

Do you have time to smell the roses?
Can you stop to watch a falling star?
Do you take time for introspection?
Imagining things from afar?

What would happen if you slowed down?
Would your world crumble at your feet?
Do you think you're indispensable?
Would you throw your hands up in defeat?

Slow down! Enjoy myriad possibilities
Present in each minute and each hour.
Slow down! You just might find yourself
Luxuriating in your own power.

Strengthening

What doesn't kill you makes you stronger!
If you don't have troubles you won't live longer,
You'll simply not appreciate
The happiness to which you now relate.

Forgetting Isn't All Bad

Remembering isn't always good,
Forgetting isn't always bad.
A memory might be something
That could make your heart so sad.
Forgetting some of the memories
May make your heart so very glad.

You are blessed with free will;
You can select the memories you retain.
Only you know which are harmful
The ones which should remain,
And those you know aren't beneficial,
From the few that could drive you insane.

At times recollections inundate us;
That may be good, that may be bad.
Discard all those unpleasant ones
Those awful ones we all have had;
Keep the pleasant ones you recall
From long ago, when you were a lad.

Concentrate on those that are happy,
Envision those which make you smile.
Your kids, your pets, your sillier moments—
You know that's more your style.
I wish I could write down all my memories—
Quite a lengthy book I could compile!

But I would only pen the sweetest ones,
The ones that still cause my heart to sing.
I'd meditate on the highlights—
I wouldn't journal everything.
Good and bad all have their seasons,
I wouldn't negate that for anything.

Life Is a Conundrum

Life is a conundrum, an enigma,
A puzzle one can never, ever solve.
Unexpected, ever changing, never stagnant;
Overall, you'll find some fun involved.

You will never get the hang of it,
It will always puzzle you;
How can anything so wonderful
Be so horrendous, too?

I find life exhilarating, liberating:
The only thing harder than learning by experience,
I've learned, throughout the years,
Is to refuse to ever learn by experience.

Still Dreaming

Do you keep on dreaming
When you're past "the age of reason"?
Do you entertain thoughts of romance
When it is long past your "season"?
Are romantic songs and poems
Just there for the teasin'?

Do the moonlight and love scenes
Stir you down to your toes?
Does warm and dreamy ambience
Make you forget all your woes,
As you fantasize and daydream
Of dark and dashing heroes?
Yes!

Thinking

Just sitting here thinking about you and me,
The state of the nation and productivity,
Immensity, propensity, and propriety;
A little of this and a little of that,
What it's like to be skinny, or to be fat.
My mind is full of a thousand things,
Houses, and mouses and diamond rings.
I'd like to stop thinking, least that's what I think,
But, I wouldn't want my mind to go on the blink!

Thinking, thinking, it's a perilous state,
Going around on a gerbil-wheel, that's my fate.
Sometimes my thoughts really make no sense,
About offense, and defense, perfume and incense.
No one can stop thinking, it cannot be done.
Nor would we really consider stopping,
Nowhere, no how, it would not be much fun!
So, sit back, relax and go with the flow.
Thinking is the best thing you have, you know!

It Is What It Is

It is what it is, simply everyone says—
I'm beginning to hate that phrase.
While it may seem comforting
When you're in a dilemma,
You can't negate the fact—things change.
Remember always, God can change
Anything, without any help from us.

Tough Love

Children are the joy and pleasure of life,
Even the few that aren't up to snuff.
Maybe it's the parent who is at fault,
Perhaps we just weren't tough enough.

They talk about "tough love" a lot
But it's easier said than done
To punish an unruly child,
Be it sweet little daughter or son.

But every wise Mother or Father
Is assured of sometimes "cheating".
Spare the rod and spoil the child
Is an admonition well worth repeating.

Puppets

We are like puppets in a traveling show—
The master pulls the strings and off we go.
He puts us away in a pinewood box, then
Brings us out when we are useful again.

Wasted Minds

A Mind is a terrible thing to waste.
You hear it said every day.
Why is it then that is just what we do—
Waste our God-given minds that way?

Romance

Mellow sax wailing softly in the distance,
Tinkling piano—the backdrop of romance.
Two hearts are turning into one,
Twirling in slow circles, as they dance.

It's a metamorphosis that only happens
Once in a lifetime, not by chance.
If it's real, only time alone will prove:
Is it true love or just a nice romance?

Don't let the music sway you,
Please be aware of propinquity.
Lonely hearts are easily influenced,
When she gazes up so ardently.

They are enraptured with each other,
Gliding around the floor so easily.
In the bright light of day that could change
Quicker than the proverbial one-two-three!

Don't pay any heed to what I say,
I'm a cynic—but an optimist!
I doubt true love, because it's been
So long a time since I've been kissed.

I still believe there *is* true love.
You just don't find it very often.
When you do, nurture it,
And everyone's heart is bound to soften.

Romance (cont'd)

Deep down, I'm a romantic soul,
And I truly believe there is still some hope.
Cultivate that optimistic attitude
And you're more likely to avoid the slippery slope.

There has always been romance,
In art, movies, theatre and a million books.
Without its influence we would be lacking
All the love songs and all the soulful looks.

Keep on keeping on, Mr. Romance,
You keep the world revolving.
This would certainly be a sad, sad place,
If our lives you weren't involving.

Car Blessing

God, bless my car and me
And all the people that we see.
Silly as this may seem to thee,
I have remained accident-free!

Project

Once I began a project that seemed insurmountable.
I thought I had the hang of it, and pushed on with a will.
Only to discover I was doing it all wrong
And did not understand it, at all.

Friendship

Extra characters that walk across my stage—
There have been so many people in my life.
Mostly they're just "walk-ons", you might say.
Some gave me joy, some gave me strife.

One meets many kinds of people in a life-time.
I wish they had all become good friends.
Perhaps, because I've traveled widely
I've kept so many at loose-ends.

There have been a couple, though,
That have really given me a lot of pleasure.
Friendship is so important to me,
And those I'll always treasure.

I won't mention them by name,
The list would be very short—but sweet.
Some have "gone on" to better things,
But their names I won't delete.

Friendship is a very special thing,
And my children I include
As we become closer through the years,
And our personalities no longer intrude.

Busy, Happy Mother

Perhaps a little weary, but humming, nonetheless,
Puttering around her kitchen, measuring, stirring, sifting,
Banging pots and pans: she's baking for her family;
And for her it's eminently uplifting!

Sweeping, dusting, scrubbing all the corners,
Cleanliness is next to Godliness is her creed;
Her greatest joy is making her house sparkle,
All for her family, and it fills a deep-seated need.

Chauffeuring, schlepping, whatever you may call it,
Grocery-shopping, taking children here and there,
Ever-going, ever-moving, seldom lighting in one place,
Always on the go, seemingly everywhere!

All for her family, she'll be the first to tell you.
For her Lord, and kids and husband always working;
Add stranger or friend into the mix, it will not faze her,
This is the life she's never, ever shirking!

What a paragon of virtue is the busy, happy Mother.
Even at the times when she gets aggravated
They are understandable and forgivable by everyone,
Because it's very clear her love has never dissipated.

Mothers and Fathers

Mothers and Fathers are put on this earth
To love and to cherish their children.
Those, who for some reason, do not
Are not worth writing about.

Don't Stand at the Crossroads

Don't simply stand at the crossroads,
Decide and forge ahead.
No one respects an indecisive one;
Determine where to "make your bed".

God allows for errors in judgment
If, perchance, you have made a mistake.
You can always return to His loving arms,
He always permits the re-takes.

Worry

All the troubling thoughts sure weigh a lot;
The cares and trials and nervous flurries;
I want so much to let them go,
I need to relinquish all those worries.

I saw a painting once, that I liked;
It depicted Jesus carrying our baggage for us.
He can, you know, and He is very good at it,
And to Him it is never, ever grievous.

The way I see it, we can let worry consume us,
Or let our past experiences and firm foundation
                in the Lord
Anchor us and chase away the worry.
Later we'll look back and realize all the worrying
                was absurd!

Dive

Take a running jump—a flying leap off a dock,
Into that beckoning lake, and dive down deep.
Not knowing how to tell the depth before you,
So, fear, into your very core does creep.

Then, up you go, popping to the surface,
"I'll never be able to take another breath," you worry,
Just seconds before you knew it was the last,
Gulping for that life-giving air we need in a hurry!

The adrenaline rush you feel when you jump or dive,
The euphoria that sets your heart to racing,
You might only ever feel it once—that may be enough,
That energizing, uplifting sensation is so bracing.

Never

Never is such a lonely word—
Not to see a loved one anymore;
Never is sometimes a frustrating word,
As in never to do something again;
It can be an extremely sad word
If you can no longer accomplish something, but then
It is also a very hopeful word:
To never have to be or do that which you hate
Ever, ever, and ever! Amen!

Cut 'n' Paste

Imagine, if you will, you run a huge computer;
You're the only one who can direct the Universe!
Life, after all, is simply a mega-system,
And, really, could you do any worse?

There! You can see a major traffic jam is happening.
Cut that blue SUV from that busy intersection.
Paste it over into the other lane and send it on its way.
That's certainly solving that problem with perfection!

You could do this all with ease, correcting traffic problems,
And they really do need solving every hour of the day.
They're not the only ones you could solve with your computer,
They're not the only things you could help just go away.

Perhaps you could clean up your home or office,
You Sort—voilà—everything is in its proper place!
Or Save it to another Disk for further scrutiny;
If it's not even useful, Delete, if that's the case.

Better use your computer for the good of man,
In any way that you deem fits the bill.
Putting things in storage, or getting rid of them that way
Is definitely more effective than Good Will.

Sadly, life just isn't like that, or anyone could do it.
Or is it? Think of Jesus as the Master Computer Tech,
Running God's universe every little millisecond.
When we allow Him, He prevents a giant wreck.

Occasionally, you are permitted to take over the controls;
That feels so good, until you Crash and burn!
You can always make suggestions and requests of Him,
It's called praying, and we'd better quickly learn!

Cut 'n' Paste (cont'd)

But it's comforting to know He can always Undo
Little or major errors you might make
With a hasty or misplaced keystroke—
Even then He can eradicate your mistake.

He is also fully capable to Restore your life
When you inadvertently hit Control/Alt/Delete!
He can make all things new again if the System crashes!
When He operates the Computer, life is sweet!

Tick-Tock

The ticking of a Grandfather clock in the hall
May be the last remaining objet d'art that makes a sound.
I still enjoy the noise it makes—sometimes a "Cuckoo"!
I feel a fondness as I listen to those tones resound.

The ticking of a clock may be nearly passé
A relic, an antique, a thing of the past.
Everything nowadays seems to be digital
Mechanical seems to be a word that won't last.

I heard one say the ticking clock keeps him awake
If such an object resides in the bedroom.
While another dislikes the battery ones
For all the light that invades the gloom.

I have a soft spot for the manual ones
There is a friendliness in the sound of a clock.
I like the fact that it is ticking off my days;
I thoroughly enjoy the music of the tick-tock.

Stops and Starts

Stops and starts and bits and pieces
Often life is made of such.
One can't always finish tasks,
What you start may be too much.

Some projects must be done in increments,
A few, perhaps, be completed all at once.
It's not always a conscious decision,
Or what everybody wants.

Learn to take things as they come
If it seems you're in over your head, maybe,
It's no crime to stop what you began,
Until it's not a chore but an activity.

You don't eat all your meals in one day,
You don't drink all your water at one sitting.
Divide your tasks into manageable bites
You're the best judge of what is fitting.

Perhaps some days you're thinking cap is crooked,
Your just not quite up to par.
Whether mentally or physically, you're just not "with it",
It's time to regroup—stop where you are.

When you come back and continue the work,
You'll find you can accomplish more than you expect.
Breaking it up seems to have simplified the process
Once again it is a pleasurable project.

Stops and Starts (cont'd)

I know it's a hard concept to grasp,
Stopping and starting isn't in your vocabulary.
Perhaps it is age that make us wiser,
Or perhaps it is age that makes it a necessity.

Some stops and starts in the middle of your work
May make your day a little bit sweeter.
Take time for a break—have some fun;
Is your work timed on an invisible meter?

If it is, you're in trouble, that's all I can say,
Your hair will be grayer, your eyes more bleary,
As you fall under the yoke of perfection,
And one day you will simply grow weary.

Take those stops and starts as a bonus, my friend,
They may be the ultimate panacea.
You may find it the answer to that you've been seeking,
Never realizing that could be part of your agenda.

If you're one who needs to finish what you begin
All in one fell swoop, as it were,
Consider the alternatives, for the sake of your health,
And, I believe you will definitely concur.

Wonky

HEALTH

Grumpies & Quarky

HAPPINESS

JOY

Efferwescent

Contentment

This is what contentment looks like—
Staying healthy but not over-exercising,
Over-analyzing,
A little compromising.

This is what contentment looks like—
Indulging in chocolate occasionally,
Eating veggies sporadically,
Not obsessed with health exclusively.

Comfort means sometimes taking rests;
Making choices with a little wiggle-room.
Not letting life rigidly consume,
Deciding to let your inner child bloom!

Taking charge, while allowing God full reign.
Knowing He knows what's best for you,
What He ultimately has in store for you,
And what you really want to do.

Spending time with friends and family,
Playing, laughing, quietly talking,
Running, strolling, happily walking,
Doing for them and never balking.

Relaxing on a sandy beach, or climbing a steep mountain,
Contentment shows its many faces,
In a sweet and tiny room or in wide open spaces,
Taking time to thank Him for all His numerous graces!

Contentment (cont'd)

This is what contentment looks like—
Being at peace within yourself,
Happy doing or on the shelf,
Always connecting to Himself!

I've done much, every single week,
And if I tell you half of it
I'm sure my eyes would leak.
But I don't yet know everything:
It's His wisdom that I seek.

Different

This is the strangest sensation.
I just don't feel like me;
A little light-headed, a little distraught,
Just not what I want to be.
Is it something I will get over soon—
That which will go away,
Or a feeling I'll have to get used to
And live with day after day?
A little weak, a bit fragile,
Just not the "me" that I know.
Should I take a pill for something,
Or simply lie down for a while?
Baby myself or push myself
And force myself to smile?
It's the strangest sort of sensation—
Not good, not bad, or indifferent.
Guess I'll have to reconcile that
From now on I'll just feel......different.

Effervescent

Bubbling, bubbling, inside of me!
I am effervescent, can't you see?
I try to always act joyfully,
The Joy of the Lord is a part of me!

Effervescent, such an exciting concept!
Some days I feel so very inept,
But when the bubbles came back my heart leapt.
For that I am always in His debt!

It's hard to believe, but even in trouble
You can always maintain that little bubble.
He can make it arise from all the rubble.
Effervescence can be created from stubble!

Euphoria

I love the word euphoria, and that's the way I feel!
Like something deep inside me is about to boil over.
It's not joy or happiness or even falling in love,
It's an inward sensation that I can't explain.

I admit, I live sometimes on feelings,
I'm an emotional more than rational type of being.
But this is more than exhilaration or even bliss
It's a jubilation that I can't seem to express.

Excitement, even rapture, might explain it
And ecstasy and joy are only part.
It's a titillating, euphoric feeling that I have,
And it consumes my body and my heart.

Excitement Within

I feel an excitement building within me,
I am not sure just yet what the meaning will be;
I just feel like a little girl swinging in a big tree:
An indescribable feeling of being free!

I'm finished with doldrums and pity party,
Instead I intend to be found laughing hearty!
I'll no more be seen as an object of charity;
Once more I'll be full of jocularity.

Something's coming, something profound!
There's a fresh wind a-blowing and joy in the very ground.
There's an air of exhilaration all around
And an aura of happiness seems to abound.

Again, I will leap once more into the fray,
To begin living life for another day;
To love and to laugh, to dance and to play,
Tho' I know that my fears I will never allay.

There's a well of anticipation bubbling in me,
Threatening to burst forth momentarily,
When the excitement culminates, breaking free,
I believe I may fly away—indubitably!

Flying High

To begin to fill in the pieces;
To mend all the broken remains
That have scattered to the far reaches;
Then sometime, somewhere, somehow,
Something or Someone finally frees us.

Flying high above the clouds,
Sundown fast approaching;
Cotton candy clouds my carpet,
Sapphire night encroaching,

Horizon stretching far afield,
Golden streaks across the sky;
From my vantage point I trace
This gigantic silver bird I fly,

The silver stars are twinkling above,
The lights of cities sparkle below;
Now it's completely dark, totally night,
We're basking now in moon glow.

Flying high with the world at my feet,
The universe arrayed from this small window,
The experience once felt I want to repeat,
And remember when I finally land below.

I'm Happy

Everything seems to be going awry,
All is not well in the world or local scene.
I could stomp and storm and rant and rave
Maybe yell and pout like an overwrought teen.

But, I tell you, and myself, I am happy.
It's all in the mind and how you face the test.
You may get beaten down, but can rise up,
And, in the doing, realize that is the best.

I remember that old song, "Be Happy"!
I sing it and take it to heart.
It is not just "mind over matter"
Or positive thinking, on my part.

Stay in the mind-set of joy and peace,
That is how the whole world sees us.
Easier said than done, I know;
But not if you stay in love with Jesus.

Blues

You may call it the grumpies or depression or the blues;
You may be feelin' Wonky or Quarky or down in the dumps;
At times you just don't feel "yourself", you know,
You may have the doldrums, the miseries, the grumps,
Perhaps you just don't know what to do with yourself:
Remember when you had the chicken pox or mumps?

You cannot explain the feelings that you have,
You feel for anyone that ever walked in your shoes.
You just can't remember what it's like to be happy,
Why do you feel this way—you've paid your dues!
You're so miserable, my friend, it isn't funny!
Rest assured, this, too, will pass—you have the blues!

Happiness

Can happiness be measured?
Can anybody know
Of all the dreams you've treasured
And just what makes them so?
Can it be measured in degrees,
Or ounce or ton or pound?
Can they say that you are happy
Or tell you when you're blue?
Who are they to say you should be,
How can they tell you what to do?
Don't they know you can act happy
When your heart has broken in two?
Can they say you really should be
When there's nothing left for you?
They say to think that you are happy
And the thought will make it so,
But they can't show you how to be
When they don't really know.
If you've never really had it,
If you've never really known,
What can you do to find it,
And how can you be shown?
And if someday you find it,
And happiness comes to you,
Can you be sure to keep it—
Do you know what to do?
Are you going to let it slip away
And do not a thing to stop it,
Or work and strive to make it stay
And do your best to top it.

Joy

A word that's more and more on my consciousness
For many months now, is, simply, JOY.
I feel it in my being, I dream it in my dreams,
I feel an inexplicable happiness I enjoy!

It comes from external circumstanced, I know,
I can attribute it to many things, and do,
But happiness is one thing, and Joy is quite another—
I know deep within my heart it has to do with YOU.

You are working deep, deep, deep within my soul.
You've been trying to break through for quite some time.
I know it's all around me, and that others feel it, too,
It's an emotion that is awesome and sublime.

Take that word and run with it with all your heart and might
You never will be sorry to embrace that word called JOY.
It encompasses all You are, Lord,
And us, whom You employ.

Lap of God

I long to curl up in the lap of God,
To snuggle contentedly 'neath His heart;
To have Him tenderly wipe away my tears,
And lovingly, patiently, His wisdom impart.

I yearn to feel His loving arms around me.
I can almost feel His hand upon my shoulder.
I know that when I am away from Him
My body, my life, my soul grows colder.

Oh, may I ever spend my time with Him,
All my days, till I'm beneath the sod;
Then nestle throughout eternity,
Resting peacefully upon the lap of God.

Crying

Crying in the sunlight, for no reason at all,
Except the beauty of the landscape is so poignant
Crying when there's just no logical reason to cry
And every reason to smile—that is my penchant.

No rhyme, no reason, not an explanation in sight,
For producing copious tears or sobbing aloud;
When I am all by myself, alone or with another,
When I am caught up in the middle of a crowd.

Why do I want to cry and sometimes do?
If doesn't always make good sense to me,
And makes even less sense to you.
That's just the way it was meant to be.

Laugh

Two sayings I'd like to review here,
They're not my words, but consider:
"Laugh and the world laughs with you",
"If you can laugh at yourself
You'll never run out of things to laugh about",
Just two of the quotes I might mention.

They are favorites of mine,
And I attempt to live by them.
It is certain that if you wail and cry
The world will surely not join you;
And no one likes a guy with no sense of humor
And a sour face, with personality to match.

I am writing this here to say—LAUGH!
Smile, chortle, guffaw, chuckle or grin.
The lines from your smiles are not nearly as deep
As the lines when you grimace and frown.
A down-turned mouth, a petulant expression
Will never get you anywhere in life or love.

If you love life, and you want folks to know it,
Then cultivate a pleasant countenance.
If you're not always so sure, and sometimes sad
A smile will help you more than them.
Maybe you think that is faking it,
But it's not—it's for your own good.

A good, hearty laugh is good for the psyche;
Try it, you'll like it, I'm sure.
Watch a funny show, or joke with a friend,
(But I'm talking about those that are pure.)
Read a good book, or converse with a buddy
Or enjoy the marvelous outdoors.

Smile

People just don't smile much anymore.
Have you noticed that, or am I thinking crazy?
Perhaps my mind is playing tricks on me
Or maybe faces all around me are becoming hazy.

People laugh—I've heard them—what a
Heartening sound to hear a guffaw, a chuckle,
A tinkling, musical whole-hearted laugh
That comes up from the toes, or belt-buckle!

But people don't seem to smile much anymore
A slight lifting of the lips, perhaps, a tiny grin,
But, generally speaking, not a genuine smile
That once graced the faces of all our kith and kin.

A smile that even lights up the very eyes
Of those who do so and it shines on you,
If you meet such a smile you are happily surprised
To note the happiness in them rubs off on you.

Smile and the world smiles with you
Isn't just a saying that you've read.
Learn to smile at people and yourself, too,
And joy in both your lives will be well fed.

"Quarky"

Some say that I'm a quitter,
I can't finish what I begin;
I'm not, I just feel it's my decision,
When I halt a task is when I determine.

You might call it attention deficit disorder,
It's not; I start and stop in my own time.
I might call a "time out" in the middle and
Go on to something else—is that a crime?

I admit at times it's hard to focus,
That's when I know it's time for a change,
Doing something different for a while,
Perhaps I just need to rearrange.

I call it feeling "Quarky"—
Not quirky, nor flaky, not in any context;
It's an ambivalent feeling that comes over me,
I am just not sure what's coming next.

I lose my confidence, get a little hazy;
It could be mental or simply age approaching.
Or that I begin a major project
And find Life encroaching.

"Quarky" is a state of mind:
A little fuzzy-headed, not quite on the page.
There's some physical aspects, also,
Unless it is all advancing age.

"Quarky" (cont'd)

Not up, not down, not good, not bad,
Not perky, nor lethargic, not at the top of my game;
A trifle lackluster, somewhat sluggish,
A little ennui, but accomplishing, just the same.

It's not an unpleasant place to be,
The middle of this "quarky" state.
So, I will accept it, for however long,
I must ponder and cogitate.

Wallowing

Sometimes there's a comfort in just wallowing.
Wallowing in old memories, in a blue funk.
Bringing up sad thoughts, sad scents, sad tunes,
Thinking thoughts of yesterdays and all that junk!

Wallowing may seem comfortable,
But it must be avoided at all cost.
It always causes repercussions;
Rebuke it now, lest you be lost.

Wallowing isn't really your friend
It results in sadness and tears,
It brings about angst and depression;
The consequence is ultimately, fears.

Wonky

You don't really feel bad,
You're not really sick;
A kick in the pants
Might do the trick,
But you might just fall over
If you really got that KICK.

You just don't feel like yourself,
Wonky's rather a disturbing feeling;
Your body just isn't cooperating
And your head is just a-reeling!

You're not sick, just a little wonky.
You're up, you're down, you're sideways,
Your emotions hit the ceiling.
Tomorrow I'll kick this wonkiness,
And that sounds very appealing!

Pill

I want to fix everything with a pill,
Which isn't always efficacious.
Sometimes if I just hold still,
Stop being so loquacious,
All the symptoms will bow to my will.
Am I being too audacious?

There may not be a pill for this.
Relax and let Him handle it.
Putting it in His hands I can't miss.
Make my prayers be more explicit—
I know that would help immeasurably.
I'd be a more effective witness.

Perky

I am enjoying good health now
And am feeling quite perky,
I might even say that
My mood is rather quirky.

My glass is half full
But it looks a bit murky
I might travel to Maine
Or to Albuquerque.

I could be talked into
Trying tofu-turkey,
But my preference would be
For eating beef jerky

Tired

I'm sleepy, I'm tired,
In my rut I am mired,
I think thoughts that are dire,
I long to retire.
How much sleep do I require
Before I am a "live-wire"?
Much more energy I need to acquire
Or my talents He needs to inspire;
I'm not ready to expire
So, I'd better get "on fire"!

Weary

I am no longer tired, or fatigued, or exhausted,
I'm just weary to my very core.
Things are asked of me that I can't deliver,
I simply feel that I can do no more.

One works and slaves and struggles
To do or be someone in this life,
Then becoming just that someone—
Someone whose life is filled with strife.

This probably sounds to you so negative,
But I never meant for it to be.
I am really happy with my life,
I am merely very weary.

It is definitely required in one's life
That he receives the rest he deserves.
Once in a while, I think, it could be too much,
That it seems to deplete one's reserves.

We must push on, persevere, continue,
As we weaken and our eyes grow bleary.
I insist that I am not distinctive,
I am just inexplicably weary.

Pity Party

I'm having a pity party
And even God is invited!
He knows that I won't stay there
Long enough to be indicted
By the overwhelming feeling
That my world is closing in;
I realize tarrying at the party
Would be akin to sin.

So, sometimes a pity party
Is what the Doctor ordered.
Cry awhile—let it all out—
Even ranting and raving may be supported.
Everyone needs a good cry now and then
And He fully understands it,
For you are never really alone—
After all, He invented it!

My Heart Never Smiled So Hard

It is an outrageously gorgeous, amazing day!
I'm on top of the world for no apparent reason!
It seems that everything in my world is going right,
I am gorging on watermelon, though it's not in season.

Simply nothing can go wrong today:
My enemies all hoist on their own petard!
It's an incredible feeling, this ebullience I feel—
My heart has just never smiled so hard!

Sometimes the rotten lemons you receive
You think you must keep—they're all you've ever had.
You roll with the punches, accept the inevitable;
Some days are good and some days are bad.

But days like this one make a liar of all that.
From morning until night, sunrise until sunset,
I skip and run, my mode of transportation is a hop
From puddle to puddle without even getting wet.

What a spectacular day this has been!
What marvelous surprises—that fifth ace is *my* card!
I am happy, attractive, filled with the joy of life!
I doubt my heart's ever smiled so hard!

There's no room for melancholy in my life,
No chance that depression will take hold today;
Happiness is uppermost in my imagination;
I sing, I dance, I feel so very bright and gay.

My Heart Never Smiled So Hard (cont'd)

Tomorrow—well, maybe; that remains to be seen;
But for now, I am basking in a time completely unmarred.
I will always have today to remember and look back on;
I know my heart has never, ever, smiled so hard!

I pray you can remember and identify with this conception.
I hope you always can look back and recall this little verse.
For each time—each day—each circumstance unpleasant
Should remind you always—things could certainly be worse!

Smile, exult, yes, celebrate each hour you've been given!
All the less-than-happy times you simply disregard.
Only bring to your remembrance those exquisite hours
When your heart just never smiled so hard!

Peaceful

We're immersed in a period of trouble and angst;
Our country, our world, is changing as I write.
I have never been a fearmonger, but I say, unequivocally,
There has never been a time in history when we might
See things quite so unusual, different, and strained.
Alarm's at every corner, like a thief in the night.

But, few times in my life have I felt this peaceful!
Everyone is pulling together and doing what they're told,
Whether trying new ways to work or sitting quietly,
For the good of themselves, their families and their world.
I salute the selfless workers, carrying on as they can,
Even when the world may seem dark and cold.

This peace of mine passes all understanding, it's true.
For the most part, I am at rest, relaxed, I can smile;
It has nothing to do with external circumstances.
I dwell on the positive when down, once in a while;
I wish everyone that peacefulness, and its Source.
I continue to experience that peace, that's my style.

ABOUT HEAVEN

From an earthly perspecive

Almost Home

My goal is close to realization,
My journey's nearly completed.
The epitome of all my expectation
Is nigh—I'm almost Home!

The culmination of all my dreams,
All I have anticipated,
The fruition of my earthly schemes
Is close at hand—I'm almost Home.

There's little more that I could ever wish,
I'm happy that the end is close at hand;
From good and bad I can distinguish;
It's all good—I'm almost Home.

It's not a time of sadness,
Nor is it a time I would want to delay.
It is definitely a season of gladness—
Heaven's my destination and I'm almost Home!

What's Heaven Like?

I wish I knew what Heaven was like,
I only know what they tell me.
No one has ever gone and come back
To say what it's like, except in a story.

At the End

When my life on Earth is finished,
And my time at last has come,
When I've completed the work He's had me do,
And my sojourn here is done.
I'll be happy to go blithely
To a new life that's begun.

I'll step joyfully into His Presence,
To bask ever in His Son.
I pray that I go gently to
Meet my loved ones, one by one.
I'll merrily sing with the angels,
And won't that be such fun!

But tears and angst and fearfulness
I know there will be none!
I won't contain my happiness,
For my reward, at last, I've won!
I'll be just like a child again,
As into the Father's arms I run!

The Way Home

Do you know the way Home?
Are your feet on the Homeward road?
Do you really know where you're going?
Are you sure of your ultimate abode?
If so, you know the old saying—
You've hit the "Mother Lode"!

Be Gay!

Don't wear somber colors
Or sport long doleful faces;
Don't hibernate alone
Or eschew gay places;
Wear red, if it suits you,
Orange, purple or green,
So everywhere you chance to be
It will clearly be seen
That my demise is a happy time —
I'm where I want to be.
I'm supping with my Jesus
For all eternity.

Not Disturbed

I'm getting closer and closer to Heaven,
And I'm not in the least perturbed.
I'm growing closer and closer to Jesus:
My faith's not in the least disturbed!

Heaven

I can't imagine Heaven without enjoying sleep,
I can't imagine any more breezes wafting o'er.
The things theologians say describing Heaven
Are to me just rhetoric and lore.

I'll imagine my own Heaven, if you please,
And it contains people and places and things I love;
I'll continue to do so most vehemently
Until He takes me to be with Him up above.

Fantasy of Heaven

I dream that someday, when I'm up there,
I'll be writing the songs for the angels to sing,
Painting the landscapes and sunsets I love—
It will all be so grand—I can do anything!

I'll do whatever God has me to do
For peace and joy and harmony to bring.
Perhaps I'll even play the guitar
And sing again, so uplifting!

I'll be able to do what I only dreamed here,
It will be all about accomplishing.
But if it isn't all to the glory of God
I don't want it! What was I thinking?

Rule and Reign

I know it says someday we will rule and reign
Over God's coming Kingdom, by and by.
I don't want to rule and reign,
That sounds like too much work for me.
I want to rest, to cease the striving,
I'd like it better to be able to fly,
To circle over this beautiful world,
To be as one with the clouds and sky.
Why must we rule and reign?
That's for young people, and so I sigh.
Just let me bask in His Presence . . .
But if that's what HE wants, I will try.

Fresh Start

I write a lot about fresh starts
And the changes that enter one's life;
The happy, the great, the encouraging ones
And those that can cut like a knife.

I love fresh starts, as I've already stated:
Mondays and moving and mornings,
I love new beginnings and starting all over—
Even events that occur with no warnings.

But I've not yet told of the Fresh Start
That's the greatest, biggest, most important of all—
The day one starts fresh with Jesus,
That's the one thing you'll always recall.

That hour when you accept Him
Into your heart and mind and soul;
All that has gone before is forgiven
And in His Kingdom you now enroll.

A fresh start, a new beginning for you.
They call it "the sweet bye and bye".
An inauguration of epic proportions,
The commencement of which we must comply.

No words can define the happiness we'll find,
At home at last with Jesus.
Sublime culmination of all of our dreams,
The moment when He sees us!

Graduation

I may be graduating soon—I can't tell.
I know I'll be going to Heaven, not to Hell.
At last, I'll achieve my doctorate, I like to think,
But this degree isn't about intelligence, and can
            happen in a blink!

It has nothing to do with what I know, or tassels on my cap,
And everything about what He knows, and imparts to me,
            mayhap.
This graduation I've anticipated all my life,
Through much travail, some heartache, and some strife.

But overall, it's been a mostly happy time.
I'll miss this old world, but Heaven will be sublime.
I'm not looking forward to a "ceremony"
Just the "going home", the rest is phony!

Perfect Balance

In heaven I won't have to wait to talk to someone
Or hear the thoughts of others I respect.
I can orate on any subject that comes to mind,
And discuss anything, on any subject;
I won't be too loquacious or have to be too quiet,
It will be the balance that I need—just perfect.

Happily Old

My body is exceedingly saggy,
My face quite alarmingly baggy,
Even my tail is ever-so-waggy;
Could it be I am getting old?

My eyes sometimes are prone to be teary,
And often they are weak and bleary;
Legs and back are growing weary,
My digits are very often too cold.

Is this called aging, in your view?
It's hard to admit it, even to you;
And sometimes, yes, it makes me blue.
'Twould be nice to just put it on hold.

But, then, I recall with gratitude,
Even a long life's just an interlude,
And thoughts of Heaven begin to intrude;
Then I will see Jesus and happily behold!

There's just one thing to say to you:
Don't wish to stay here past 82,
But be joyful and happy, if you do!
Copy me, if I may be so bold.

My Friend

My friend, I really miss you,
All the good times that we had;
The many times you dried my tears,
In the times that were so bad;
The things we went through together,
The laughs, the angst, the fears,
Even the times we did not agree,
So few, but some, it now appears.
Mostly, I did not agree for you to go.
Your time on earth was fleeting.
But deep within my heart I know
That Jesus you'll be greeting!

Secure Future

I'm closer to You than I've ever been before.
I feel in tune with nature and with You.
My past is far behind me,
My future is obscure.
But in one thing I am confident—
That future is secure.

I'm convinced my future is secure—
The problems of today, I know, will be
The solutions of tomorrow.
There is only peace and joy ahead of me
I'm joyfully anticipating eternity,
I'm finished with all sorrow!

I'm Sorry

To apologize to one that you once loved—
Perhaps it is never really too late.
Even now, with an ocean under the bridge
I may never know if it was God or fate.
I can blame it on your past baggage
Or possibly just too little, too late.

I can say that I'm sorry for your angst.
I know our children were products of love.
Whatever we did, right or wrong
They were our gifts from God above.
I wasn't the best wife in the world,
You weren't the perfect mate the world speaks of.

All was forgiven some time ago;
I pray the same thing can be said of you.
But there is a sorrow deep in my heart
That God alone can say is true,
That we were not mature enough to make it work,
And I'm very sorry that I hurt you.

I'm trying to recall the good times—
I remember most the tears;
The memories are not so very sweet
Regretfully, I remember the fears.
I don't know why that had to be—
Just a few sweet things in all those years.

I'm Sorry (cont'd)

There's something radically wrong with that.
If you'd told me of your past, your trauma,
Maybe I could have understood you more,
And we wouldn't have had all the drama.
Had we been more mature, we might have made it,
But, in reminiscing now, it's all a gray panorama.

I'm sorry—it might have worked out
If we had both been born-again.
Oh, we were, but many years after.
It doesn't matter if it was one year or ten.
I'll look you up and say, "We done good, Kid!"
I'm ever-grateful I will see you Then.

Ribbons

I'm bound to earth with ribbons, not chains.
All an enterprising angel needs to do
Is to slip up behind me and untie the bow
And watch the ribbons fly up to the sky
And let this earth-bound body simply—go!

The ribbons are so pretty and so colorful,
They've bound me for so many, many years;
They're silky-soft and flutter in the breeze;
I've loved their anchoring to this life.
They yet permit me to go where e'er I please.
But now I'm prepared for that Great Untying.
I'm ready at long last to loose the ribbons
And allow my once-bound body to be free
To soar on wings of angels to my ultimate reward.
Where I will finally utterly, completely just be Me!

Packing My Suitcase for Heaven

I'm packing my suitcase for Heaven!
Oh, I know, it's a bit premature,
But I always tend to pack early
Whenever planning a trip in the future.

If going to Aunt Clara's or Grandma's
Or a trip to an Alpine resort,
I pack at least three days early:
I wash and I mend and I sort.

This time I'm packing important stuff:
My Robes of Righteousness, for a start.
And then, there's my Garment of Praise;
Of course, I will throw in my heart.

All my love I will take Him
And all of the works I have done.
After all, He's my source and salvation
I owe all to the Son.

You say it's a little too early?
Well, you know, there's no time like the present,
To pack and prepare and be ready,
'Cause I never know when I'll be sent.

I'm packing my bags for the Big Day
Anticipating it so joyfully;
I'm packing my suitcase for Heaven,
'Tho' I know I can't take it with me.

I'm Still Me

I don't do the things that I used to do,
Nor look the way I wanted to,
Nor act the way I should,
Nor even think the way I would.
    But I'm still Me

Time changes almost everything—
The way I walk, the way I sing,
The thoughts that people have of me—
Perspective is all, you see.
    But I'm still Me.

The color of my hair has changed,
My avoirdupois has been rearranged,
My lips have even thinned a bit,
And my body—well, go figure it!
    But I'm still Me.

I am the same inside as I used to me,
And intend to be through eternity,
Tho' they say our bodies will certainly change
As in Heaven a new one we'll exchange:
    But I will, innately, still be Me.

Petition

Am I, somehow, transmitting my thoughts to you,
          my friend?
Our hearts and minds were once so closely attuned
That I pray you can feel me now,
Sending my thoughts and my tears through the miles,
Wanting so desperately for you to know,
In your last hours on earth, that I'm thinking of you.
And so, praying for a peaceful transition
From this vale of pain and tears
To that perfect world in Heaven,
Where you'll be so warmly welcomed by Him,
And your son and your beloved husband,
And, I'm sure, Mom and Dad have been waiting
          for you—
You made them wait a mighty long time!
That was for our sake—you are so well-loved
And such a prayer warrior—par excellence!
God couldn't have accomplished quite so much
          without you.

My Dear, I will miss you, though I haven't seen your
          smiling face
Or heard your sweet, sweet voice in many, many years.
Yes, we kept in touch for quite a while—
Then one day, neither could no longer, by telephone,
But I wrote to you and kept our friendship alive
And, I know, you kept me in your heart.
You just kept on, praying and working for the Lord.
Your heart just wouldn't stop its beating
For us, for your family, for your multitude of friends.

Petition (cont'd)

You will be so sorely missed—you are already!
Your children, grandchildren, even friends you didn't
                know you had
Will grieve, because we're all so selfish
Not to realize you're heading for much better things.
God's given me the assurance that your place with Him
                awaits.
You'll hear Him say, "Well done, good and faithful
                servant,
Enter into the joy of the Lord!" and you will smile.
I pray you can feel me reaching out to you right now,
And are aware of all the tears I'm shedding,
Mostly, because I can't be with you in your hour of need.
But, in reality, I cannot do anything for you but pray.

Bride

I don't want to think of Heaven right now,
I have far more mountains to climb.
I have more fish to fry and people to meet,
One more painting, one more rhyme.

There's a thousand things I need to do,
And hundreds of books to read.
Millions of thoughts I need to think,
Many gardens I need to weed.

But I don't want you to think I'm not prepared.
I'll quietly and happily go there one day;
I'll be grateful I know where I'm going,
And my bridal dress will be my array.

I have my wedding dress all prepared
To be the Bride of Christ.
He has paid for the cost of my finery,
Sadly, it all was overpriced!

Requiem

Don't hold a Requiem for me,
Go on as if I'd never been.
I expect you'll shed a tear or two,
But please, don't create a big scene.

I don't expect wailing and gnashing of teeth,
No long-winded speeches on what and where,
Or even one of those songs that I love—
I am not there.

I'm walking hand in hand with the Saints,
Basking in the light of His Glory,
Fellowshipping with loved ones gone before me,
Relating to each other our life story.

I'll be laboring with Him to create a new Kingdom;
One day you'll be with me, just the same.
We can work together ever after,
Always for the Glory of His Name.

Don't mouth foolish platitudes
When my time has come to leave the Earth
And I'm no longer there with you in person.
Know that I'm experiencing my own re-birth!

Please don't sing a Requiem over me;
Rejoice for me, and know that I am happy
To have finally shuffled off these mortal coils.
I am not sad. Why should you be?

Practicing Praise

A friend said to practice my praising,
'Cause someday that's all we will do.
I do want to be obeying,
And to be praying and praising anew.

But I just can't conceive of not "doing"!
Being silent and still is not me.
I know neither praising nor praying
Is ever best done quietly.

Then, I realized they are both "doing"!
But my body won't be at all weary
When I'm praising my Savior up there,
And my eyes will not be all teary!

So, I'm happy to pray and to praise Him,
But if there's something else He wants me to "do",
I'll be more than happy to oblige Him,
And always do what He wants me to.

Sleeping

They say there's no sleeping in Heaven.
If not there, it's implied, in the Word.
But, please let me sleep up in Heaven;
Never to allow that would be absurd!

Sunshine in Heaven

I truly hope Heaven has lots of sunshine,
And delightful breezes galore;
High-flying birds, without the poop and the pecking,
Beautiful flowers, without bugs, around my door.

Don't give me that argument on moon and tides;
I just don't want to think that way.
I know science is true and nature is nature,
Just let me indulge in my daydream today.

As in Camelot, the rain and snow only after sundown,
And the darkness isn't so Stygian—one can see—
It's not so threatening nor depressing,
But friendly, warm and welcoming to me.

Each cloud in the sky will be fluffy and white,
There may be puppies and kittens, but allergies, not any.
There will be music and dancing
And our voices will be melodious again.

I know the light of Jesus' face
Will be the sunshine in Heaven,
And the lack of all I've mentioned here
Won't really be a burden.

I can only relate to things of earth
In imagining what it will be like there.
So, for now, I'll envision these wonderful things,
But when I arrive there I won't care!

Visitation

Hello, My Friend:
Yes, your eyes do not deceive you,
Though you're seeing with your heart.
God knew you wanted to see me
Since you couldn't see me depart.

Gaze upon my countenance,
Note the joy that fills my face;
I knew you had to see that
To receive closure—to grief erase.

Although you cannot hold my hand,
Nor touch my smiling face,
You can sense my arms around you
And feel my warm embrace.

We are salt-sisters, after all,
As close as a marriage vow.
I have your back and you have mine—
That still continues, somehow.

No, I'm not here to beckon you
To come with me today.
You need to do what He has for you.
I just came that I might convey

The love and peace and joyfulness
I'm undergoing as we speak.
To see you again in the flesh, as it were,
Our relationship has been so unique.

Visitation (cont'd)

You know I was buried in my wedding gown,
My reasons most won't comprehend.
I am truly, now, the Bride of Christ!
For me it's the beginning, not the end.

Please have a cup of coffee on me
And a hot fudge sundae, of course.
I've fought the good fight all my life
So, I have no remorse.

Goodbye, My Friend, I'm going now
But you'll feel my presence forever.
For every day, as long as you live
You will most likely be reminded of the "Weather".

Train to Heaven

You've heard it said and sung,
'Bout boarding that heavenly train;
You'll need no wallet or baggage
You'll not be returning again.

The conductor will call your station
As you approach that Pearly Gate.
You'll be welcomed there by Jesus,
For you have long-since sealed your fate!

From Fear to Joy!

Yea, though I walk through the valley of the shadow of death
I will feel no darkness, no evil, no angst, no fear.
Although I am about to depart from the earth I love
And all the precious people that I hold dear,

I know He is reaching out to hold my hand in His
And hold me tight, no matter how it may appear.
I know I am in Him and He inside of me.
I am assured that very soon His voice I'll hear.

And those of all my loved ones gone before,
I anticipate the joy of holding one another near.
I can't even imagine how magnificent it will be
Experiencing an eternal, brand-new frontier!

Ultimate Security

What do you do when one you love
Is approaching that Last Mile?
Rant and rave, cry and scream,
Or, possibly, merely smile?

Smile, for you know where they're going;
You are certain their troubles will end.
They'll soon reach the Ultimate Security!
What more could you wish for a friend?

ABOUT HIM

Inspirational — Motivational

God-Centered

Aftermath

Is it really an aftermath, or is it afterglow?
They are really quite different, you know.
That which occurs after a momentous event,
Or the euphoria of a time well spent?

I prefer to think of it as afterglow
But aftermath works, too.
Whatever you term it, it's the same—
Not wanting something to end.

Like a beautiful dream you wake up with
And just can't seem to "get out of".
You want it to go on and on and on
Like a symphony by Rachmaninoff.

The afterglow extends throughout your life
After you've come to know the Lord.
Every day seems sweeter and sweeter
When you plug into His Word.

One day you won't need to conjecture,
Is it aftermath or afterglow—
Are you happy because you belong to Him?
Or because you know that you know that you know?

Arise as Pure Gold

In Job, after all his trials and travails,
He insists, "I will arise as pure gold!"
That's the attitude we all must have:
We must have confidence, and be bold.

We must not let all our problems
Make us whine and wallow in defeat;
Me must rise above circumstances
And, ultimately, the Devil cheat.

We must have faith and trust in God
To bring us out of grief and despair;
No, it isn't easy, but we are overcomers.
Someday into His eyes we will stare!

If we but persevere until the end
We will one day Him behold.
We were meant to stick with Him;
We will yet arise as pure gold!

Lead Me Straight to Prayer

Every word I read and write about
Each tiny little word
Leads me to its Author
Leads me to my Lord.

Broken

Do you ever feel so broken
That even God can't fix you?
You know the Original Manufacturer can do it
But you can't even believe it's your due.

You feel that the warranty has expired,
That you're on your own in this life;
Hope is hope but broke is broke,
And you're beyond repair.

You don't know what brought you to this state
Nor when that first crack appeared;
You tried paste and glue and mortar,
But you're just too far gone, you feared.

Well, know that's a lie from the devil!
He wants you to give up and fall apart.
God can and will and wants to fix you,
But you have to allow Him to start.

Trust God

There are so many things I want to say
So many things that I want to do.
I trust God to tell me what He wants me to say,
And show me what He wants me yet to do.

God Laughs

Don't you sometimes hear God chuckling in the breeze?
Or gurgling in the rushing mountain stream?
Or laughing right out loud in a cheerful sort of way,
When a summer storm blows up from out of nowhere?

Can't you just see Him smiling fondly at the antics of
                    His children;
Or the sweet, sad smile when we are naughty?
Oh, I know some think of God as a serious, sober statesman,
Ruling o'er the earth with reign of iron,

Coming down on all of us;
With a frightening fury when we dare step a
Fraction out of line—not me!
I know I often hear God laugh.

I know my God is awesome, but His rule is not by fear.
He's a loving, gentle parent, wanting only what is best
For me and everyone concerned.
And I can trust Him to take care of me.

As with my earthly father, my uppermost desire
Is to do whatever makes Him smile.
I cherish every moment that in precious camaraderie,
Not only can I hear God laugh, I know He laughs with me.

How I love to hear God laugh!

Cross

There's a Cross around my neck
And a Cross upon my wall;
A Cross in my heart, as well.

Off *my* Cross the Lord has long since come down:
The Resurrected Christ lives inside of me
The devil to dispel.

The Cross can be just a "figure of speech"
Or impact one's life mightily
And fill every sinew and cell.

Don't minimize the Cross
Or maximize the symbol:
It will assuredly keep one from Hell.

Keep close to your heart
The true meaning of the Cross
And all fear and angst 'twill repel.

Desperate

Take the word, "desperate".
I think it says it all.
It says more of our relationship
With Jesus than any word I can recall.

We all are really desperate—
But we don't have to be!
We can know Him now, this hour,
And for all Eternity!

Can't Pray?

At times, perhaps, we think we cannot pray;
Too busy or too full of other things.
Maybe we just don't know how or what to pray
Or we're afraid of what that prayer brings.
But if we really, truly, know Him,
If we are friends with Him in every way,
It is no longer just a conscious act on our part,
But a reflex action, some might say.
And then, there's many times the Holy Spirit,
Without our thinking, oft He will relay.

Doubter

Hey there, Doubter, what are you doing?
You know who I AM but your doubts keep accruing.
You've loved Me for a long time,
You've accepted Me for the upward climb
Yet still you are a Doubter, and that's not the thing to do.
Hey there, little Doubter, what makes you think it's cool
To have a niggling little doubt? That's more than being a fool!
You can't believe Me one day and then doubt Me the next;
You are exceedingly inconsistent, and with you I'm very vexed!
So, tell Me, little Doubter, what you intend to do.

God Surprises You

It's funny how God comes along behind you
And bolsters you up when you're down.
He's always near to comfort you
And make a smile of a frown.

He oft' holds your hand when you're shaky;
You feel His presence supporting you,
Making you happy when you could be sad,
And joyful when you should really be blue.

You trust in Him, but it still comes as a surprise
When He's suddenly blessing you!
It's amazing how God surprises you
When you least expect Him to!

Wisdom

The wisdom of God is a marvelous thing!
Just ask anyone who's achieved it.
Solomon, in Proverbs, speaks much of this
And we all would do well to heed.

Covet His wisdom, discern what He means,
Then go out and convey it to others.
It is not very much good to keep it all to yourself
He expects action from sisters and brothers!

Experience

I've experienced depression
So, I can write about it;
I've experienced joy and sorrow
So, I'm pre-approved to shout it.
He's allowed me to go through everything
So, when I relate them you won't doubt it.
Hear me now, and listen well
As I presume to spout it.

I've been there, done that, over it.
I know whereof I speak.
I'm older than the hills, you know,
And done much, every single week,
And if I tell you half of it
I'm sure my eyes would leak.
But I don't yet know everything:
It's His wisdom you should seek.

Experience is not necessarily the best teacher.
The Holy Spirit is better, by far.
He can tell you of things you know nothing,
Of life and problems unpopular,
All the "how-to's" and "why-nots" and such
Explaining Chopin and Renoir
I can't do that if I tried to
But that's just the way things are.

God the Father, the Son and the Spirit
Exist so you needn't experience
Everything there is in this world;
They can give you a pretty good sense
Of the circumstances you are experiencing
If you heed them and don't become dense.
Then you can pass it along, to help others:
They're always with you, for your defense.

God Shouldn't Have Invented Temptation!

Why in the world did God invent temptation?
However did He think that a mortal could comply?
He made us to be fallible, didn't He?
He never made us perfect, so why, oh, why

Did He ever expect a mere mortal
To not succumb to temptation or defy
The Tempter, when he was on a roll,
Thinking up temptations that could make one cry?

God should never have invented temptation,
For we are so weak and find it hard to obey;
Even when there is no such thing as temptation
We stumble and fall on any—make that every—given day;

We find we cannot be perfect or even come close
To the standard He's set for us in every way.
Guess the answer is accepting Christ Jesus:
Then we can scoff at temptation and hold it at bay.

Complete Trust

There are so many things you want to say,
So many things you want to do;
Trust God to tell you what He wants you to say,
Trust that He'll show you what He wants you to do.

He's in Everything

Good times, hot sex and hot showers,
Gorgeous sunsets and lovely flowers,
Sitting with a loved one, hours and hours,
I know He is the one that empowers.

Mountain streams so clear you think of infinity,
Sky so blue you're reminded of the Trinity.
Awe-inspiring poetry, art or music
Beauty, inspiration, so intrinsic.

The magnitude of the ocean, the sky
Can only produce heart-felt sighs!
So many things I've come to love
But nothing so great as the Lord above.

I've come to believe He's in everything
Big and small and all in between.
From the smile of a beloved
To the wave of a Queen.

Nothing is too insignificant for His approval
Aware of every sense and moment and feeling
Nothing's too infinite that He doesn't know it
It has to—it must—send the mind reeling!

I cannot conjure anything He isn't in charge of,
My finite mind just cannot imagine:
A kiss, a prayer, a hug, a hum, a hymn,
No matter how trite, horrendous or stupid,
He is in everything!

Hold Me

Put Your arms around me, hold me tight.
Let me put my weary head upon Your shoulder;
I've never had much experience with this scenario,
But I miss it even more now that I'm older.

I pray, I seek Your countenance, but I yearn
To feel Your arms tightly encompassing me.
Am I merely preparing for that Ultimate Meeting
When You will hold me for Eternity?

Sometimes I just don't feel quite well
And long to feel Your Presence covering me.
Sometimes I'm in the middle of a "Pity Party"
And need to know You love me unconditionally.

Mostly, there's no rhyme or reason for this feeling
That I simply want to cry and hold onto You.
It's irrational—but that's how You made us,
So we would always keep running back to You.

So, hold me, Lord, e'en when I cannot feel it:
Put Your loving arms around me, hold me tight.
I always feel Your love surrounding me,
Holding me tenderly through the darkest night.

Could it Be Now?

Could it be now
That we hear the first blast of the trumpet,
That we see the lightening of the eastern sky?
Could it be now
We see the first glimpse of Jesus
Stepping out upon the clouds on high?

Are we ready to receive such a sight—
The blazing sun splitting the night?
Are we really ready to meet Jesus?
Will we rejoice when first He sees us,
Or fall prostrate on our very faces,
Feeling unworthy to accept His graces,
Appalled that we have not done what we should,
Or even all the things we genuinely would?

Could it be now?
Can we conceive of it?
Are we looking upward with joy
To anticipate this ultimate climax
To all that we have thought and prayed
And dreamed of since we met Him?
Could it be now?
Even so, Lord Jesus, come.

If the Foundation be Destroyed

If the foundation be destroyed,
What, then, can any do?
Swept off our feet, washed away,
What can there be, in lieu?

What we believed and trusted in,
Everything that we once knew,
Comes crashing down upon our heads;
To faith we say, adieu.

The lessons we had all been taught,
The beliefs we've held since birth,
Are now in dust beneath our feet,
Crumbled into the very earth.

Faith, Hope, Love, Joy, Charity,
There is now a shortage, nay, a dearth,
Nothing's good now, nothing's bad,
There is naught left of any worth.

If the foundation be destroyed,
We would be undone, forsooth!
We would never know of Jesus,
And never know the Truth.

There's a sermon in there somewhere,
But I'll let another preach it.
I pray you'll listen and take heed
While a better one than I doth teach it.

I Asked the Lord

I asked the Lord for something that I wanted
And He said, "I gave you life!"

I asked Him for a gift to better serve Him,
And he answered "I have given you great gifts.
You need to discern them, then to use them."

I asked the Lord for a word in season,
That I might give it then to those in need.
He replied, "You have My Word—
Accept it; read it; live it; share it!

Head or Heart?

We blithely sing about it,
And write about our impressions,
And contemplate all we have read;
But do we truly believe it all?
Has it gotten into our hearts?
Or is it, after all, just in our heads?

Nibbling

I take the Bible and nibble at it,
Word or passage or line;
I tend to grasp it little by little,
To read large sections I decline.

At times I devour whole chapters and books,
I seem to be insatiable.
Sometimes I don't read it for days at a time,
But to not read it at all is untenable!

Whether you read it a word at a time
Or take it in gulps, sips or swallows,
Know that He's leading you all the same:
It is just as the Lord allows.

Travelers

Every man is a traveler,
Seeking his destiny.
If he would but pause in his traveling
To open his eyes and really see!

See that Infant Jesus, now become
The Savior of us all.
And then he could cease traveling,
Stand still and heed His call.

Traveling may be good at times;
Far better to sit at His feet;
To commune with this simple Majesty
Is what makes one complete!

I Will Not Fall!

I will not fall away from God
I will not fall away.
I am of "the elect", they say,
But I will not fall away!

I will remember all the joy
That my salvation brought to me;
I will go back to the beginning
When I first fell on my knees.

I determine not to leave You, Lord.
Let not your Spirit fall from me.
Grant, I may diligently seek Your face,
Blot out all my iniquities.

Let It Go

Do all you can to obey His will for your life
Overcome all the turmoil and strife.
No one person, be it husband or wife,
Knows all the solutions or all the strife.
Some may destroy, cut like a knife.
After you do ALL you can in this life
Let it go!

Temptation of Jesus

Was knowing He would never have a lover
Or an earthly family, difficult for Jesus?
Were such temptations common to Him as well as us?
Does that, in any way, change the way He sees us?

The Bible says He was tempted in every way as we are.
Does that mean, although we're never told, explicitly,
That He, too, had dreams of love and even sex?
That He once longed for a loving wife and family?

I wonder what Jesus thought about in the stillness of
                    the night.
Did He always concentrate on what He knew to be
                    His Destiny?
Oh, I believe He was perfect, but wasn't He even once
Tempted to be a little less than what God wanted
                    Him to be?

They say He was a comely man, and certainly,
                    good and kind.
There must have been some women who vied for
                    His attention.
He had to have been appealing to them;
His single status must have been a bone of contention.

We can spiritualize Him all we want—and should!
But at one point in His life He was a sought-after bachelor.
The Mary's and Martha's and a nearby shepherdess or two
Surely flaunted their considerable allure.

Temptation of Jesus (cont'd)

It's obvious He never succumbed to temptation,
But He had to have had some trouble with lust.
Was that the "thorn in the flesh" He passed on to Paul?
I'm sure He entertained some thoughts He had to adjust.

It's proven by the fact that Satan,
At the infamous trial in the wilderness,
Tested Him in many ways, but
Had no need to tempt Him with lustfulness.

This is all just to say that our heroes are just men.
Pedestals are made to fall off of.
God fashioned us all equally flawed:
It's not the temptations, but the rising above.

If even Jesus could be tempted,
And no one is sure whether He was or not,
Then who are we to feel so superior?
There's always a trap in which we might be caught.

And if we're ever good and truly caught,
He has made a way to overcome.
Granted, it's not easy to rise above it,
But I know it can certainly be done!

There Was a Reason

There was a reason you chose to take my baby boy
Although he hadn't time to even live.
The man I loved left way too young, and early—
He seemed to have yet so much to give.
There was a reason.

You called a teen-aged grandson home,
I know not what he had in store.
My Mom and Dad and siblings, too,
They all have gone before.
There must have been a reason.

And yet, I'm here, I've hung around—
It profits me not to even conjecture.
I do not know Your reasons I'm still here—
I'm too short-sighted to comprehend the big picture.
Sufficeth to say, You had a reason.

I can but thank You that Your reasoning
Is always, ultimately, for my benefit;
I'll one day understand Your perfect plan,
If only just a very little bit.
I trust that You had a reason.

Only He

Only He can know the torturous thoughts I'm having,
Swirling 'round and 'round my baffled brain.
Only the Spirit deep within me knows their meaning;
I fear no clear thoughts ever will return again.

Only He could possibly have any idea
What I am truly trying to convey.
My tongue's too tied to speak coherently.
Oh, thank You, Holy Spirit, for the words I say.

At times there's only one way to express myself—
My Heavenly Language many times it's called.
I cannot know how I must pray for someone,
Only He knows—my feeble brain is stalled.

Only He—the Father, Son and Holy Spirit
Will always know how I must communicate;
If I am still and simply let Him have His way
It's always worked for me, at least to date!

I'll Still Believe

Many Christian songs have been penned
Regarding my favorite Bible verse,
That now I'll paraphrase and retrieve:
I know my God will deliver me—
But should He not, I will still believe!

Strength

The Bible tells, in many places
That God will give us strength.
In Deuteronomy He promised Asher
He'd given him strength to last his days.
I find that oh, so, comforting
As my physical strength is ebbing
I claim that promise for myself
To carry me through my years and days.

In Job He promised him his latter days
Would be more rewarding than the former
He knew what Job had need of
And granted him much, much more.
I believe He wants us to claim
These promises of old.
In this day and age, they are still true
We can sense it to our core.

Oh, not so much the physical strength
Are we entitled to receive,
As much as mind and spiritual strength—
May we always have the mind of God.
I know that He has told me
That this is what He has for me,
And, as for all the gifts He's given me,
I heartily applaud!

Strength seems such a simply word
When one is twenty-two,
Both mentally and physically
We take for granted what we had.
It could be we were never all that strong
But we were the best that we could be
That's just what it was and wasn't bad.

Strength (cont'd)

Now we're striving for more inner strength
More a "hold-on-to-the-end" kind of thing,
A "do-what-you-can-when-you-can".
We know that He plans for our very best.
So, we keep on pushing on to the "higher things"
And doing the very best that we can,
Until one day we are given our rest.

Specific

Be specific when you pray,
Don't "pray around the world", as they say.
Pick a prayer and pray about it,
Then prove to Him that you don't doubt it.

You'll be amazed how specific He can be,
When He answers so explicitly.
If, perhaps you don't see it immediately,
Rest assured He is working on it expediently!

Not in this Life Alone

I'm not in this life alone,
Tho' I have much for which to atone.
I've got a partner, a helpmeet, a friend,
Who'll stay by my side e'en past the end.

I know I am never without a comforter,
Without a confidante, a helper,
I cling to His hand as He helps me along;
I am happy, contented, filled with song.

I'm not by myself, existing on my own,
I am never in this life alone.
I will always have His calm assurance
To uphold me and provide endurance.

I may be perceived as being a solitaire,
But it's only an illusion, for He is there.
He gives me peace and joyfulness,
I know I need accept nothing less.

If I could convey one truth to you,
I pray that I actually could imbue
The reality that has become my own:
In this life you are never really alone.

On Time

Never too little, too late, nor too early,
He's always on time, no matter how it seems.
If He doesn't always feel "on time" in your life,
It could be *your* expectations, *your* dreams.

The first thing we are taught to believe
Is, "Thy will be done";
Why do we argue or chomp at the bit?
Are we really prepared to argue with the One?

Reconcile yourselves to that great truth:
He's always perfect in His timing,
He's not a poor poet,
Imperfect in His rhyming!

Reward

What in the world does a person do
Who doesn't know the Lord?
How can he possibly hold it all together
Without delving into the Word?
How can he go on living and breathing
Without brandishing the Sword,
And without the assurance of Jesus,
The certainty that He always sees us—
Knowing Heaven will be our reward!

Top Priority

I yearn to be someone's "Top Priority",
But having never been that, I'm confused.
Was there ever anyone who thought I was that special
Was there ever a time I didn't just feel "used"?

Am I making this up? Over-exaggerating?
Crying the blues for no reason?
Was there one period of time this wasn't true,
Did I ever enjoy "my season"?

There must have been a time, at least a day
When I was all-in-all to someone.
I couldn't have existed my whole life
Not ever having anyone!

I'm making this up, this just isn't true,
I was once important to someone!
It just doesn't feel like I was ever "Top Priority"
To a husband, parent, friend or son.

But enough of this pitiful poem!
I know I'm Priority One
To the One who made the universe
And that's certainly the best Someone.

Prayer List

My prayer list changes from day to day
Sometimes, even, hour to hour.
But the best are those I pray on the spot,
That their grief He may devour.

When God Is Silent

I have learned to enjoy when God is silent.
I am confident He is planning something fabulous.
His mind is always set on me, His child,
And His works are continually marvelous!

Yes, there are times He doesn't answer,
God has been silent at times, I know.
It is then that He's backing up for a running start;
He is pondering where He wants me to go.

When God is silent He is busy thinking
Of making me happy and ways to bless me.
Or, perhaps, He is wondering how to explain
That chastisement is in order—He does that, you see.

When God is quiet He has not forgotten,
He simply doesn't choose to talk right now;
He has other, more important things, to do.
But, rest assured, He'll get back to me, somehow.

I have been angry and I have asked, "Why?"
I have ranted and railed at Him, too!
I have doubted, distrusted, even defied
And still He never gives me my due.

I would deserve any punishment He could devise;
I do not deserve all of the blessings He gives.
He is all-patient, most loving and wise.
He maintains it is just because He lives!

Where Are You?

God, where are You in the deep, dark night,
When I cannot sleep for whining?
I have everything that I need in life
And still You find me pining
For things I think I have to have,
Like fancy houses or fine dining.

A figure to knock someone's socks off,
And a wardrobe so enhancing;
A choice of shoes and high heels,
So, I can go on dancing.
No, I don't want to be a femme fatale,
I'm not one that wants to be entrancing.

Lord, I don't really want any of those things
And still I pray for my lack.
Why are humans made to yearn
For things, and then, just take them back.
We vacillate between the good and bad
Only sometimes we are on the right track.

Why don't we really know our own hearts,
Why don't we even know our own minds?
We want to be good and honest and brave
We turn out to be the other kind.
Are we always going to be so ambivalent,
Do we constantly have to live in a bind?

Where Are You? (cont'd)

Paul said it for us in Romans 7:15:
I want to do good but I don't;
I want to live right but I won't.
The things that I do
When not thinking of You
Are the things that I don't really mean!

God, where are You, in the dark of the night?
Where are You in the heat of the day?
Change me, mold me, make me more like You;
Rearrange my thoughts and actions today,
Stay by my side, lead and guide me
Every minute, every hour, every day!

Thank You

Thank You is such a little word!
It doesn't say enough
When saying it to my Savior
For answered prayer when life is rough.

I just cannot communicate
All the gratitude that's in my heart.
How do you thank Someone for saving you?
I simply can't enunciate.

Thanks is insufficient
For miracles when life was tough.
It's just so inadequate!
Thank You, Lord, is not enough.
But I must try!
Thank You, Jesus!

No Fair

'No fair!" he shouted, shaking his fist at God.
'No fair!" like a little boy wanting his own way.
Life just wasn't treating him
The way he thought it should.

"Life isn't fair!" she cried, when all answers seemed to be "No!"
"Nothing's going the way it should.
I say my prayers and do what's right,
I *know* that I've been good!"

He might have just refused to pay our ransom:
"No fair!" He could have cried in the Garden of Gethsemane.
He could have told His Father, "They're not worth it!
I can't endure that cross at Calvary."

Now, can you still cry out, "No Fair?"

Loving Me

You must love me very much!
I am not unaware of Your sacrifice—
You suffered and died for me.
My simple words will not suffice!

I simply cannot conceive of Your great love;
It is incomprehensible to my finite mind
That a perfect Savior could care so much—
For such a love all my life I pined.

Until I finally realized I had it all the time,
I only needed to accept it as mine.
It was then I gave my life to You,
And You showed me Your love as a sign.

I can't express what You mean to me;
I am grateful that You paid the price.
But I won't fully conceive of Your love for me
Until I confront You as my Christ!

I must live as though I mean what I say,
I must be what You want me to be,
I will try as diligently as I can
And love You back, for all eternity!

READIN' WRITIN'

....NO 'RITHMETIC !

Agonizing

Am I simply writing poems,
Making rhymes as I go,
Extolling the virtues of Jesus,
Or is it heart-felt—I don't know!

Am I so caught up in wording,
Trying so hard to rhyme,
That I've lost the true praise and worship
That I've strived for all the time?

Sometimes it seems like smoke and mirrors—
I'm not conveying what I truly feel.
Can I stop writing to please others
And attempt my heart to reveal?

I ask, I beg, I beseech Him
And pray in the Spirit, as well,
But does it all reach him?
I suppose only time will tell.

I am led to consider Elijah.
The Lord visited him of old.
He, too, sought a sign from God
And His answer is there retold.

Perhaps He's saying to me now,
"Take heed, I have made my choice;
Not in the wind or earthquake or fire,
I'll answer in a still, small voice."

Agonizing (cont'd)

So, whisper now to me, Lord.
It all seems so much to consider.
I've weighed all the pros and cons, it seems—
Should I go with the highest bidder?

That doesn't seem to be what You're saying.
Why is Your voice so unclear?
Are my ears too stopped up to hear aright?
My intellect is no help, I fear.

I must be still and listen,
Only then will it all be made known.
Speak once again in that still, small voice,
Drown out that of my own!

Make crystal clear Your will to me,
Let it come as a revelation,
And, then, at last, I'll hear plainly,
And my heart will be filled with elation!

One More Rhyme

'Til just before the end of my days
I'll always have one more rhyme in me.
There will always be another poem
'Til just before I meet my Destiny.
I'll still have something to convey,
To leave for posterity.

Journaling

Now, I'm really reaching for poetic subjects, it seems,
But everything I do, think, or experience
Lends itself to another couplet or two.
Perhaps I am simply "journaling",
It's just the way I deal with life,
In case someone ever wants to know what I do.

I can rhyme about my stapler, and my computer
Is a favorite subject of mine, as well.
I write about my feelings, my passions, my dreams,
I wait for inspiration and He writes for me.
I tell of my "I wishes", "if onlies", and my prayers,
And all my plots and plans and schemes.

I'd like to write some unforgettable sonnet,
An epic poem that everyone would spout,
That would go down in history as my legacy;
But that, most likely, would not be what He wants.
I just write as he leads me and what I am told,
And trust Him that it's not all lunacy!

Dwindling

My poetry seems to be dwindling down.
Haven't written a word in many a day.
Oh, I could still pen a verse with a word of your choice,
But inspired subjects are fading away.
Perhaps because I am so self-absorbed
And am, in fact, slowly dwindling away.

Rhyming

The life of a poet is unrelenting,
Time after time I think this is the last;
But, then, another thought I must jot down
About my present, future or past.

Free verse does nothing for my psyche—
Yet, rarely, I, too have succumbed.
But I do believe that genre
Must "sing", so to the depths I've plumbed.

I read the works of other poets;
Some I wish I'd written in my time.
My favorite mode of expression will always be
The lines that spill across the page in rhyme.

Writer's Block

I thought "writer's block" was just for novelists,
But now I've found it applies to poets, too.
It may be applicable to a bard or versifier,
If a rhymer goes for weeks without a rhyme or two.
They bemoan the fact there's not a current poem
While I'm not usually one to force the issue,
The best way to get beyond the "block"
Is simply to begin—I know it's true!

On Reading

When I read about "The Little Matchgirl"
My fingers are frozen to the bone.
Reading about the Chicago mob
I think of Al Capone.

I sigh such heartfelt sighs
When re-reading "Wuthering Heights";
And when I'm perusing etiquette
I take such dainty little bites.

Immersed, perchance, in "Peter Pan',
I empathize with those Lost Boys.
Enjoying "Jo's Boys" and "Little Men"
I tend to smile at all the noise.

I can sympathize with all the tragedy
And not with a sense of ease,
Identifying with the characters
When reading "War and Peace".

While reading a tender romance
I'm caught up in a whirl.
And in all the patriotic passages
I seem to see the flags unfurl.

I cannot ever read horror stories
Because I am too easily scared.
But love and even philosophy
To them my soul is bared.

On Reading (cont'd)

My favorite genre is comedy—
I really love to laugh.
Happy, sweet, light-hearted fare,
But not the raunchy ones, by half!

I like to live in a world of make-believe—
Books and stories take me there.
It is so much better than real-life
But it's fiction—I'm truly aware!

Lists

I sit here in my chair making list after list
Of things to do and things I'd like to do;
Tasks I really need to accomplish
And probably I will

But it will take me 10 times longer
Than once it used to do.
I make out endless grocery lists
And stuff to buy some day,

And lists of what I want to do
When I have the time and the money,
And lists of those to call and see
Whenever I get the energy.

If I spent the same amount of time
Doing these things instead of making lists
Everything on my To Do list
Would already have been Ta-Done!

Our Crazy English Language

Oh, our crazy English language!
This will take more than a minute.
The homonyms, antonyms and synonyms
And so very much more in it.

Nock is the notch in an arrow,
And knock is a rap on the door.
Or knock is to disparage something—
One word can mean so much more.

How about those digraphs—
The sound of a consonant pair,
Like "th" and "ch" and so forth,
You find them everywhere..

What about the "ou" sound?
These diphthongs will be the death of me!
Rouge and rough, though and slough
Thorough and through—that's enough!

What about see, and sea and si
And sow and sew and so?
The sea that's not always water
And a favorite of mine—so-and-so.

How can a foreigner to our shores
Hope to learn the English language?
And yet so many do so well
Even indulging in badinage.

Our Crazy English Language (cont'd)

You usually can tell one born elsewhere
And educated in our language over here.
They speak more distinctly, with a better vocabulary
And to our English rules adhere.

Perhaps the secret is, just trying
Harder to learn and respect our language.
We've gotten lazy and sloppy
Treating it all like extra baggage.

Let's vow to not be so apathetic
Toward a language that's really swell.
To learn a new word once in a while
And not simply blurt slang out pell-mell.

A word is a wondrous thing;
Learning new ones is truly a joy.
Being brave enough to admit you've pronounced
          something wrong
Is good for a girl and a boy!

Hooray for the English Language
And all of its strengths and shortcomings;
Its foibles and faults and weaknesses
Still keep us from being such dummies.

Mail Call

If you've ever been in the Service
Or been a missionary, far away,
You know the importance of Mail Call,
The brightest spot in your day.

If you've ever been away at school
Or far from that certain someone,
Watching for the mailman every day
Is just not very much fun.

Then when you're older and home-bound
Mail Call's the height of your day.
Whether it is a package you sent for
Or a note from a friend with something to say.

Mail Call is very important—
Sometimes you just live for that time.
It's like having Christmas all over again—
Mail Call can be so sublime!

Penchant

This penchant for rhyming is compelling,
I seemingly operate in automatic,
I need another bit of doggerel as I need
The sunshine—and I'm frantic.

I write and write to no avail,
Except to keep my nimble fingers moving,
And my engorged brain is constantly
Spewing out so something I'll be proving.

I'm not at all sure what it is, exactly,
That sends my fingers flying o'er the keys;
But I'm grateful for the talent God gave me—
Sometimes it actually brings me to my knees.

I've said it often before, I write because I write;
And until I can't, I will continue
To bombard my friends and family
With my rhymes—that's what I do.

Why I Began

I write because I love to write.
I write because I need to write.
Almost everything I experience
Suggests a rhyme or two.
I've written poetry, now, for many years
I jot down notes whene'er I can.
About a thousand poems later
I'm wondering why I began?

Winging It

Tonight, I'm simply winging it,
Free-wheeling, if you will,
Writing that which pops into my head,
Whether or not it fits the bill.

Rhymes about all sorts of things,
Pain and aging and sadness.
Lines of "what if?" and "if only"—
That road leads to madness!

For the most part I know why I'm writing
And where my mind and pen are wending;
Invariably my thoughts are optimistic
And usually have a happy ending.

Sometimes I simply feel like rambling;
Writing what I feel like writing.
No real reason or forethought,
Just whatever sounds inviting.

Most likely, it won't be important at all—
Often just trite and silly;
But if it comes to my mind, I know it's from Him.
I write with Him, not willy-nilly!

Truth in Poetry

Be true to yourself when you're writing,
And not simply think of your audience.
A poet must always write what he feels,
Not merely consider the ambience.

Rambling

There are so many subjects for poems
They are everywhere I gaze.
I could write about any and everything
And that could fill my days.

I've written of staplers and edible eggs
And emotions and feelings and such
I can't even imagine a subject remains
Yet there still remains so much.

I simply need to be writing.
To pen a verse every day
Because I never stop thinking
There's always a new thing to say.

So, before I start rambling on and on
With nothing much to convey,
I'll stop, for now, and come back to it
And rhyme again another day.

Little Rhyme

A rhyme a day keeps the blues away,
A poem is part of my makeup;
A verse, I say, keeps the doldrums at bay,
And, oftentimes, cures a breakup!

Praying on Paper

At times you just can't verbalize a prayer
All your words disappear into a vapor.
Then it's good you can pray in the Spirit
Or simply, pick up your pen, and pray on paper.

My thoughts and prayers are more succinct
Organized better with a computer or a pen.
I seldom see a piece of blank white paper
That I don't dredge up all thoughts that have been hidden.

I just realized that's what my writing is—
Every word is a prayer to You
My poetry, my journaling, a letter to a friend
Are really simply notes to You.

I know that all I do is God-ordained,
But I really, really get it now, although,
I really don't know why it took me so long
To realize this and go with the flow.

Praying on paper is what I do.
   That is what I will continue to do.
      That is what I am meant to do,
         For myself and You!

Paying Homage to the Book

I'm a very tactile person—I'm the touchy-feely sort.
I love to touch your spine and caress your face;
Your back is just as smooth as your cover,
Your interior is simply impossible to replace.

You can have your little Kindles and your phones;
All the devices they're reading on, everywhere you look.
I enjoy the smell of paper, its gloss and shine and all—
I love the feel and texture, the smoothness of a book.

There's no substitute for the written word
On paper, book, note or tract.
I love a textbook, a classic or a paperback.
You cannot be replaced, and that's a fact!

Yes, you can underline and highlight, extract, delete
When using a computer to study and such,
But there's one thing you can never do—
You can never, hold and touch!

Bits of Paper

I have an obsession for writing on
Little pieces of paper, everywhere:
Reminders of when to do my nails
And when to cut my hair.

Papers with a name upon—
Friends I owe email or letter;
When to send a Get-Well card
To hope they're feeling better.

I always jot down a word or phrase
I would like to add to my book;
I have phrases upon phrases laying around
Wherever you may look.

Someday, no doubt, I'll glance and see
A bit of paper, there it lies:
With my name written on it,
And the date of my demise.

Rhyme My World

I really see a rhyme in everything around.
A spider, or an octopus or water on the ground.
Palatial homes, small houses, and country abodes,
City streets and highways and winding country roads.

Animals, vegetables, rain and snow,
Bright summer with the sun all aglow;
I love to rhyme my time away,
It helps to keep the blues at bay.

A Little Bit More

I just can't seem to stop writing,
So, I'll write a little bit more.
Thoughts and ideas simply keep coming;
I never know what He has in store.

Every time I think I am finished
God opens another door.
I just have to keep rhyming,
I feel it to my very core.

Bits and pieces and thoughts and words
Keep bombarding me all the time,
I simply cannot stop;
I'm beginning to think in rhyme.

I go on and on ad infinitum,
Even when my head hits the pillow;
I conjure up rhymes like some count sheep,
Peccadillo, armadillo, weeping willow?

Most of it isn't important,
A lot of it is truly nonsense.
But I love to smile and I like to laugh,
Even at my own expense.

Bear with me as I'm winding down;
I'm trying diligently to finalize
This little tome of mine,
And still remain healthy and wise.

Inspiration

Inspiration comes in very small smidgeons
Or huge chunks of verbiage, some of the time.
Who is to say which will be the better poem;
I cannot say which makes a better rhyme.

I think of a silly, inanimate object and take off
With a dissertation that's more of a jingle.
Something momentous happens in my life
And my words and thoughts make me tingle.

I can tell that they are all inspired by God,
'Cause from where else comes my imagination?
I love imagining all sorts of things;
At times I even think in rhyme and syncopation!

I've always wanted to put my words to music,
But, I guess I'll have to let another do that.
The music remains, though it's all in my mind;
It keeps buzzing around in my head, like a gnat.

Inspiration's a fickle creature, though.
It comes and goes very willfully.
And it doesn't matter if you ignore it,
Or weave sweet words so skillfully.

It is what it is, and I do what I do,
To please Him, and myself, to stay busy.
I need the exercise of my fingers and mind,
Although sometimes I get dizzy!

So, I'll continue to invite the inspiration
On every level I may receive it.
To the end of my days, I'll delve into His ways,
And put pen to paper, as I perceive it.

A Small Thanks to the Medical Community

You are the pillars of the community, the world.
You are the unsung heroes in this period of devastation.
The heart, the brain, the compassion, the empathy
Are all appreciated by a grateful nation.

We can stay in our little houses
Away from the turmoil and strife,
But you are all on the cutting edge;
You know what it's like in real life!

If we never appreciated our medical workers before,
We apologize. We won't take you for granted again.
We will forever extol your virtues,
As long as it is within our ken.

This doesn't say enough, but Thank You,
You're heroes, each and every one.
From the janitors to the neurosurgeons,
You will continue until it is done.

Salute to ALL

I wish to salute all those who are "carrying on as usual":
police, firefighters, health care workers, postal workers,
retail, food industry—to all, actually—everyone who
is experiencing the trauma and the differences during
this terrible time, enduring the Covid-19 pandemic
in our nation and our world! Yes, even those of us who
merely stay at home and write about it! "They also serve
who only stand and wait!" -John Milton

The Author

Printed in the United States
By Bookmasters